The Temptation

Also by Theodor Reik

The Temptation

THEODOR REIK

GEORGE BRAZILLER · NEW YORK

1 9 6 1

Grateful acknowledgment is made to E. P. Dutton & Co. and Everyman's Library, for the quotation of eight lines from "Hebrew Melodies" translated by Margaret Armour, from PROSE AND POETRY by Heinrich Heine.

To My Son Arthur

CONTENTS

: 7 :

Prelude: The Beginning

THIS BOOK is in the great tradition of research launched by Freud, my master and friend for thirty years, and it continues his investigation in a certain direction. This direction has an early association with a statement Freud once made to me during a conversation.

I was then a young and inexperienced psychoanalyst to whom he referred some cases of neurotic disturbances. It often happened that I would run into him on his evening walk in the streets of Vienna, and I would eagerly use the opportunity to discuss the difficulties I encountered in my practice and to get his advice. On such an occasion I expressed my astonishment about the attitude of a patient whom Freud had sent me. The young man showed a determined resistance to speaking of his childhood and boyhood years, and evaded every possibility of remembering events of his early life. Freud attentively listened to my report and said: "A man who is not at all interested in his past is a ne'er-do-well." I was surprised, nay, I was shocked. Freud hardly ever pronounced moral judgments. When he did this time, it was only because it was in an informal conversation with one of his youngest students. He was right in this particular case, as the development of the analytic treatment proved during the following months. The patient was a psychopathological character, bordering on the criminal.

I had been inclined to contradict Freud's statement because it seemed to me that it was an unjustified generalization. I have since learned that a complete emotional break with one's past, a willful taking down of all bridges with one's own history, has certain unfavorable characterological consequences. Freud mentioned in that conversation a proverb (if memory does not fail me, Roumanian): "What you run away from follows you." This is valid for an individual as well as for a people. Whoever disavows his past suffers some damage in his personality.

A few years after that conversation my thoughts became preoccupied with the study of prehistoric rites and religious practices. My research, later published as *The Ritual*,[1] tried to penetrate the earliest and fundamental presuppositions of religion and society. In the preface to that book Freud states that its author "keeps steadily in view the relationship between prehistoric man and primitive man of today." This principle determined also the character of certain books, published in the following years, dealing with problems of primitive religion and prehistoric civilization. Then followed an interval of almost forty years during which I was occupied with different problems of psychoanalytic psychology. Returning on a long detour to the questions that had interested me in my youth, I published a trilogy[2] dealing with unsolved problems of Israel's prehistory.

The work here presented continues this line of research. It too belongs to the realm of archaeological psychoanalysis, as I called the new and undeveloped branch of depth psychology. It approaches the archaeological and anthropological material from psychoanalytic viewpoints and tries to reach the hidden core of prehistoric Hebrew society and religion. None of these researches is undertaken with the design of systematic exploration. They are rather adventures in psychoanalytic discovery. The methods of depth psychology are here only applied as new tools of investigation, comparable to those of dendrological, carbon 14 and obsidian tests, used in modern archaeological work. Some early hunches were followed and examined, several of which proved mistaken or had to be modified. Others, however, could be verified and supported by intrinsic evidence.

In following and examining significant leads, one enjoys all the excitement of reading a detective story. Yet there is another emotional element connected with work of this kind: a sense of moral commitment. (Or is there, in this zeal, a concealed desire to come closer to our forefathers before we are gathered to them?) It is as if an inner unrest cannot be mastered until the challenge of those prehistoric problems is met.

Pedestrians in the streets of New York sometimes stand suddenly before a group of workers who take up the pavement and dig down into the ground as if they were in search of hidden objects. On the sawhorses encircling the deep hollows in which those men are working are inscribed the words: "Dig we must—for growing New York." Similarly, dig we must—for growing understanding of the past.

THEODOR REIK

New York, June 1961.

PART ONE

THE
CHALLENGE OF
THE PROBLEM

AND IT CAME TO PASS *after these things, that God did tempt Abraham, and said unto him, Abraham: and he said, Behold, here I am. And he said, Take now thy son, thine only son Isaac, whom thou lovest, and get thee into the land of Moriah; and offer him there for a burnt offering upon one of the mountains which I will tell thee of.*

GENESIS XXII:1,2

CHAPTER I

Prologue

— ❦ —

W HEN YOU STAND BEFORE the building of the Jewish Theological Seminary on New York's
Broadway, you will read above its portal the
inscription, "And The Bush Was Not Consumed." This
line from Exodus (III: 2) serves as a symbol of Jewish destiny and survival. When you go up to the library of the
institute on the first floor, you are confronted with a life-
sized reproduction of Rembrandt's wonderful painting
"The Sacrifice of Isaac," a picture of an interrupted ritual
of human sacrifice. That Biblical story is of high signif-

icance for the spirit that pervades the Judeo-Christian civilization, the spirit of the Lord who says, "I desire kindness and not sacrifice."

It is with that story that this book deals—but not only with that story. I assert that the secret meaning of the myth reported in the twenty-second chapter of Genesis has not yet been recognized and that its traditional explanation just scratches the surface of the legendary material. I believe that the investigation here presented reaches the primal shape and unearths the subterranean meaning of the myth. It is in this respect comparable to the reconstruction of a prehistoric sanctuary undertaken with the help of archaeological findings. Tracing the myth back to its roots is not undertaken for its own sake, but as a means of attaining some insights into the still-unknown religious and social life of the ancient Hebrew tribes.

The writers of the Holy Scriptures end the general history of mankind with the story of the Tower of Babel and the subsequent dispersion of the people. From there on the narrative restricts itself to the form of a series of biographies. It deals with the adventures of the patriarchs of nomadic herdsmen who roamed from place to place searching for fresh pasture.

The Old Testament's survey of ancestors opens with the biography of Abraham, who is the first person to be called a Hebrew (Gen. XIV: 13). The first patriarch looms as one of the great figures in the history of Hebrew religion. He is the father of the faith and has the distinction of being called "the friend of God." There is no doubt that this biography as told in the Genesis narrative is a combination and condensation of many single stories —some of them only much later centered around Abraham—stories first transmitted in oral tradition, often remodeled and reshaped, elaborated and finally completed. The story of the arrested sacrifice of Isaac is one of those tales:

And it came to pass after these things, that God did tempt Abraham, and said unto him, Abraham: and he said, Behold, here I am. And he said, Take now thy son, thine only son Isaac, whom thou lovest, and get thee into the land of Moriah; and offer him there for a burnt offering upon one of the mountains which I will tell thee of. And Abraham rose up early in the morning, and saddled his ass, and took two of his young men with him, and Isaac his son, and clave the wood for the burnt offering, and rose up, and went unto the place of which God had told him. Then on the third day Abraham lifted up his eyes, and saw the place afar off. And Abraham said unto his young men, Abide ye here with the ass; and I and the lad will go yonder and worship, and come again to you. And Abraham took the wood of the burnt offering, and laid it upon Isaac his son; and he took the fire in his hand, and a knife; and they went both of them together. And Isaac spake unto Abraham his father, and said, My father: and he said, Here am I, my son. And he

said, Behold the fire and the wood: but where is the lamb
for a burnt offering? And Abraham said, My son, God will
provide himself a lamb for a burnt offering: so they went
both of them together. And they came to the place which
God had told him of; and Abraham built an altar there;
and laid the wood in order, and bound Isaac his son, and laid
him on the altar upon the wood. And Abraham stretched
forth his hand, and took the knife to slay his son. And the
Angel of the Lord called unto him out of heaven, and said,
Abraham, Abraham: and he said, Here am I. And he said,
Lay not thine hand upon the lad, neither do thou anything
unto him: for now I know that thou fearest God, seeing
thou hast not withheld thy son, thine only son from me.
And Abraham lifted up his eyes, and looked and behold
behind him a ram caught in a thicket by his horns: and
Abraham went and took the ram, and offered him up for a
burnt offering in the stead of his son. . . .

"So Abraham returned unto his young men, and they rose
up and went together to Beersheba; and Abraham dwelt at
Beersheba (Gen. XXII: 1-13, 19).

The Biblical scholars generally attribute the tale almost
entirely to the source "E," as they call an editor or a
group of editors who use the expression "Elohim" as
divine name. Those editors are to be dated around 800
B.C. and located in the Northern Kingdom. Only a few
verses (15-18, 20-24) are attributed by the scholars to the
older main Biblical source which calls God by the name of
Yahweh. The verses 15-18, perhaps later inserted, say

that the Angel of the Lord "called unto Abraham out of
heaven the second time and said 'By myself have I sworn,
saith the Lord, for because thou hast done this thing,
and hast not withheld thy son, thine only son: That in
blessing I will bless thee, and in multiplying I will multiply thy seed as the stars of the heaven and as the sand
which is upon the sea shore, and thy seed shall possess the
gate of his enemies; and in thy seed shall all the nations
of the earth be blessed; because thou hast obeyed my
voice.'" These verses glorifying Abraham's obedience
and repeating the promise of the Lord given to Abraham
are out of place and are artificially tied to the Isaac story
by a thin thread.

The Biblical account is not the final version of the
temptation of Abraham. Few of the Old Testament stories have given birth to such an abundance of additional
legends as the tale of Isaac's sacrifice. Those legends are
mostly to be found in the Haggada and they are contained
in the Talmud and the Midrash. They appear in these
books among the commentaries to the Bible and amid
stories, lore and legends. Heinrich Heine once wrote of
the Haggada to which the Talmud student, weary of dry
speculation, turns for refreshment. The poet calls the
Haggada "a curious garden blossoming":

> Where the beautiful old saga,
> Legends dim and angel-fables,

Pious stories of the martyrs,
Festal hymns and proverbs wise
And hyperboles the drollest,
But withal so strong and burning
With belief—where all resplendent
Welled and sprouted with luxuriance.[1]

Solomon Goldman's unfinished study of the Bible opens with the sentence "The Book of Genesis is the great clearing which the fashioners of the Jewish saga made in the jungle of primitive folklore."[2] That clearing has been enlarged and transformed into the "curious garden" with which Heine compares the realm of the post-Biblical Haggada. In contrast with the Scriptures the atmosphere is full of ease and serenity. Yet there are some dark corners in that garden and quite a few secret paths lead into the primitive world around it. Some stories are charged with the hushed intensity of the jungle which surrounds and sometimes invades the garden through which we will now contemplatively stroll.

On the Fringes
of the Saga

HE POST-BIBLICAL LEGENDS about the near sacrifice
of Isaac, which comment on, elaborate and em-
broider the Genesis narrative, reach from sober
interpretations and paraphrases to fantastic explanations,
from rabbinical exegesis to fairy tales.[1] The mighty river
of Semitic folklore did not run dry when the Scripture
was brought into final form. It rose and swelled with trib-

utaries coming from different sides, and it slowly flowed into the outlet of modern Biblical exegesis. In some ways this body of modern exegesis is not less fantastic than the old sagas.

Abraham is, of course, the protagonist of the Biblical tale. Isaac plays only the role of the obedient son. In quite a few post-Biblical legends the character and actions of Abraham are copiously described, but in most of them the part of Isaac becomes more important than it is in the Biblical story. New characters emerge and the old parts are sometimes filled by other actors. There are changes in casting, as well as new parts. Sarah, Isaac's mother, appears frequently in dialogue. At several decisive points of the plot a new character appears: Satan, the Tempter, steps on the stage, speaking and acting. The angels are heard and even the part of the animals is not neglected in the drama.

In this chapter, I will draw from the rich source of post-Biblical tradition contained in the Talmud and in the Midrash. It would not be germane to the purpose of this study to enumerate and quote from all the legends and commentators in those sources. I will therefore consider here only those legends that serve the purpose of this exploration. The first task of our investigation is to restore the primal oral tradition from which the first written record of the Biblical Isaac story evolved more than a thousand years later. Yet the restoration of that forgotten and submerged oral tradition is not our final aim. It will provide only the means to reach and explore the pre-patriarchal phase of Hebrew religion and organization.

We begin our survey of the fragmentary legendary material with the tale of an argument between Isaac and his older brother Ishmael. The older one once boasted to Isaac that when he was thirteen years old the Lord commanded Abraham to circumcise him, and Ishmael joyfully acceded. Isaac answered him "What dost thou boast to me about—a little bit of thy flesh which thou didst take from thy body?" If, said Isaac, the Lord should command their father Abraham to bring Isaac as an offering before Him, he would not resist. Thus Isaac was tried before Abraham was. He went through, so to speak, the rehearsal of a test. It is relevant for our purpose that in this tale a comparison is made of the ages of Ishmael and Isaac at the time of their circumcision. Is it perhaps even more important that this operation—performed when Ishmael was thirteen years and Isaac was eight days old—is put into relation with Isaac's anticipated sacrifice. We don't know what the relation is, but it is significant that in the discussion of circumcision reference is made to the test that took place later.

Even the first sentence of the Genesis narrative became a subject of rabbinical exegesis. The rabbis asked, "What does it mean that the Biblical story starts with the sentence 'And it came to pass after these things, that God did tempt Abraham'?" The unlearned reader assumes that the sentence places the event after those recorded in the previous chapter. According to the authorities "after these things" can also mean "after these words." The Midrash rabbi assumes that "after these things" refers to a time when Abraham had been soliloquizing and came to realize that after Isaac's birth he had rejoiced and made others rejoice, yet had not offered anything—"neither a corn nor a ram as sacrifice to the Holy One. . . ." It was then that God tempted Abraham and demanded the sacrifice of his beloved son.

Another version is given by Rabbi Jochanan who speaks in the name of Rabbi Jose ben Zinna. In this version "After these things" refers to a dialogue between the Lord and Satan the Tempter. The legend explains how it came about that God tempted Abraham. The Lord would perhaps not have tested his servant if He Himself had not been tempted by Satan. At the banquet celebrating Isaacs' birth Satan turned up in the disguise of a beggar asking alms. No one paid attention to him. When the sons of God presented themselves before the Lord, Satan appeared among them. And the Lord said unto Satan, "From whence comest thou?" And Satan answered, "From going to and fro on the earth and from walking up and down on it." And the Lord asked Satan what he had to say concerning the children of the earth. The adversary answered that he had seen the people—they serve the Lord when they require something, but when they receive it they do not remember Him any longer. Thus Abraham once served the Lord and proclaimed His name to all the children of the earth, but now that his son Isaac has been born to him he has forsaken and forgotten God. Since then he has neither built altars nor has he brought up any offering to Him. The Lord then said of His servant Abraham, "There is none like him on earth, a perfect and an upright man before Me. . . . As I live, were I to say unto him: Bring up Isaac thy son before Me, he would not withhold him from Me, much less if I told him to bring before Me a burnt offering from his flocks or herds." Satan took the Lord at His word: "Speak now unto Abraham as thou hast said and thou will see whether he will not transgress and cast aside thy words this day."

The analogy of this legend with the introduction to the Book of Job is too obvious to be elaborated on. In this "Prelude in Heaven" to the drama of the patriarch, it is likewise not God but Satan who originally wishes to tempt one of the children of the earth.

Other legends report that God appeared to Abraham in a dream to demand the sacrifice of Isaac. According to the Koran, also, the patriarch received this divine order in a dream. The Lord said to Abraham "Take now thy son," but Abraham pointed out that he had two sons and did not know which one to take. God answered, "Whom thou lovest." Abraham replied, "I love this one and I love that one." Only then did the Lord say that he should take Isaac as burnt offering. Abraham was still evasive, and expressed his doubt that he was fit to perform the sacrifice since he was not a priest: "Ought not rather the high priest Shem do it?" But the Lord decided that He would consecrate Abraham and make him a priest as soon as he would arrive at the destined place of the sacrifice.

Some legends say that Abraham was worried about how he would separate Isaac from his mother. The patriarch explained finally to Sarah that Isaac was now grown up and had not yet studied the laws of God. It was high time that the youth should be brought to the priest Shem, who would teach him to know the Lord and to pray to Him. Sarah reluctantly admitted the necessity of instruction for the adolescent boy, but asked her husband not to let Isaac stay long away from her, "for my soul is bound within his soul." Sarah then kissed and embraced Isaac and spent the night with him weeping because of the separation. She pleaded with Abraham to take good care of the beloved boy and not let any harm come to him. She accompanied them on the road, and when she was told to return to the tent she wept bitterly. She caught hold of Isaac and held him in her arms and embraced him and said weeping: "Who knowest if I shall ever see thee again after this day?"

According to other versions Abraham did not say a thing to his wife. He rode away with his son at dawn to spare her the grief of separation.

At this point, it is essential to emphasize that Sarah appears here in the role of the mother grieving about the separation from her son. She is filled with anxious foreboding: will she ever see him alive? It is natural that the question emerges: How old was Isaac when he was offered as a burnt sacrifice to the Lord?

The rabbinical authorities do not agree about the lad's age at this critical time. Josephus gives his age as twenty-five years, a Mishnah on Genesis as twenty-seven or twenty-six, Targum Jonah as thirty-six, some other sources even as thirty-seven. Ibn Ezra points out that the reason for the rabbis' increasing Isaac's age is their wish that he be fully responsible at the time of the event. Ibn Ezra admits that we have to accept the rabbinical statements as a matter of tradition, but raises an argument on theoretical grounds: If Isaac had been thirty-seven years old he would actually have been handing himself over to his own slaughter, and his reward would have been double that of his father. His merit would have been revealed in the

Bible, but nothing in the Scripture is to be found indicating that he had earned the greater commendation.

The most rational supposition, Ibn Ezra thus argues, is that Isaac was about thirteen years old and that his father took him by force and bound him against his will on the altar. Tho proof for this supposition is that his father kept the secret from him, answering his question by saying, "God will provide a sheep." Had Abraham said to him, "Thou wilt be the burnt offering," he probably would have run away. There are other arguments for the probability that in the oldest tradition of the saga Isaac was at the age of puberty, but Ibn Ezra's rational explanation is of special importance in our quest.

It is noteworthy that Satan reappears in the role of the Tempter in some legends, where he tries to prevent the patriarch from offering the sacrifice. In some sagas Satan appears to Sarah in the figure of an old man and asks her where her son went. Sarah answers him: "He went with his father to study the Torah." Whereupon Satan declares to her that Abraham took his son on the road to sacrifice him. "In this hour Sarah's loins trembled and all her limbs shook. She was no more of this world."

In another version Satan told Sarah that Abraham had built an altar and had already sacrificed Isaac. She believed him and cried bitterly saying, "O my son Isaac, my son, O that I had died this day instead of thee!" She remembered how she reared the boy. Her joy in him has now turned into mourning. "Now hast thou served this day for the knife and the fire." She made inquiries about Isaac till she came to Hebron, and no one could tell her what had happened to her son. The figure of Sarah in her grief reminds us of the figure of another mother crying and mourning her son who died as a sacred sacrifice to the Lord.

Abraham and Isaac were accompanied on the road by two young men, Ishmael and Eleazar. In the Biblical story the young men have only an episodic role, but they are more important in some legends. In this legend they were left behind with the ass when Abraham and Isaac reached their destination on the third day of the journey.

On the road Satan appeared to Isaac in the figure of a young man—apparently of the same age as the other two—and asked him about their destination. Isaac answered him that the journey was undertaken to bring him to a place where he would be taught the Torah. "Will you receive this instruction while you are alive or after your death?" asked Satan mockingly. "How can one be instructed after one's death?" replied Isaac. "You son of a pitiful mother!" cried Satan, "don't you know that your old, silly father brings you to the slaughter? Don't listen to him!" But Isaac was loyal and rebuked Satan. The words of the Evil one did not, however, leave him unaffected, and he asked his father about them. Abraham told him not to pay attention, for they were the suggestions of Satan.

According to other legends Abraham himself was subjected to several temptations by the Prince of Darkness. Satan approached the patriarch in the figure of a very old and humble man, who said to him, "Art thou silly or foolish that thou goest in thine old age to slaughter him who did not commit any violence, and wilt thou cause the soul of thine only son to perish from the earth? Dost thou not know and understand that this thing cannot be from the Lord? For the Lord would not do unto man such evil, to command him, go and slaughter thy son." Abraham recognized that the words he heard were those of Satan, and rebuked him.

Later on, Satan, who saw that he could not prevail, transformed himself into a mighty brook across their road. When Abraham, Isaac and the two young men reached that place they tried to pass the deep water, but the water rose until it reached their necks. Abraham again recognized Satan's work and rebuked him and continued the journey, taking Isaac to the place which God had told him. While they walked along, the son asked his father "Here is the fire and the wood but where is the lamb for the burnt offering?" (According to Philo

of Alexandria, Isaac cried when he asked this question.)
Only then did Abraham tell his son that the Lord had
chosen Isaac for a perfect burnt offering instead of a
lamb. Isaac was ready—more, he was even eager—to be
sacrificed and assured his father that there was not the
slightest resistance in his heart.

When Abraham built the altar, his son helped him to
arrange the wood upon it. Then the submissive Isaac asked
the patriarch to hasten and slaughter him. Isaac was also
concerned that he should be properly bound because
when he would see the slaughtering knife in his father's
hand he might tremble and, being young and vigorous,
push against Abraham. He adjured his father to hurry
in order to fulfill the will of the Creator. He asked only
that his ashes be placed in a casket in Sarah's chamber.
Whenever his mother would enter this room, she would
remember her son and weep for him.

At this point of the narrative when Abraham had
bound Isaac on the altar and braced his arm to slaughter
him, the legend shifts the scenario again to Heaven. At
the moment when the patriarch took his knife to slay
his son, God spoke to His angels pointing out with ap-
probation the unconditional loyalty of His servants. The
angels, however, burst into loud weeping and accused
the Lord of having broken His covenant with Abraham.
We know that the patriarch was on the side of the angels.

It will surprise us to learn here that the angels were on the side of Abraham—occasionally against the Lord Himself.

The tears of the angels falling upon the knife prevented it from cutting Isaac's throat, but his soul had escaped from terror. When the Archangel Michael cried out, "Abraham, lay not thine hand upon the lad!" the patriarch released Isaac. The boy, revived by the heavenly voice, stood upon his feet and spoke the benediction "Blessed are Thee, O Lord who quickenest the dead!"

In the legends it is reported that God pointed out the ram to Abraham, who slaughtered the animal, sprinkled its blood upon the altar and said, "This is instead of my son and may it be considered as the blood of my son before the Lord." In some tales Abraham sent his son to the teacher and priest Shem, with whom Isaac stayed three years to be instructed in the Torah. In other variations Abraham returned with the three young men to Beersheba.

With the vision of Isaac's symbolic death and resurrection, we now take leave of these legends for the time being. We will return to the cycle of the tales soon, because they contain unrecognized traces of old, forgotten saga material of the ancient Hebrews. Some of these vestigial features are older than the oral tradition on which the Genesis narrative of Isaac's sacrifice was founded. There were in the pre-Abraham tradition quite a few features which the late narrators of Genesis did not like or did not want to acknowledge. Some of this material was denied or brushed aside and was picked up by the tellers of folk tales. Yet those side lines were once the main lines.

CHAPTER III

The Comments of
Theologians and
Exegetists

THE STRANGE EMOTIONAL IMPACT of the Elohistic story of Abraham, told with great economy of means, has held readers ever since ancient times. The Genesis narrative in its word-sparing eloquence has awakened admiration from both the pious and the unbeliever. Luther remarked that one feels sheer terror in the story. (*"Timor ipse pictus est."*) Scholars have pondered the problems of that chapter, great painters have presented the scene of the trial of Abraham, and poets have put it into verse. Rarely will this Genesis narrative fail to elicit praise for its diction and its religious significance, its simplicity and restraint. The narrator, says Solomon Goldman, "leaves the reader to picture for himself the terrible agony" which the divine command must have produced in Abraham, "the rude blow to his natural affections, the dismay at the prospect of losing a son upon whom all his hopes and aspirations for the future were centered."[1]

Other commentators speak of the "poetic halo which has been cast around one of the most startling, yet appealing chapters contained in the historical portions of Holy Script."[2] John Skinner, who calls the narrative "the literary masterpiece of the Elohistic collection," comments on its exquisite simplicity: "Every sentence vibrates with restrained emotions which shows how fully the author realizes the tragic horror of the situation."[3] Goldman, as well as many other commentators, points to the many anxious questions to which the conflict of motives must have given rise in Abraham.

A recent writer, Dorothy B. Hill, wonders if it is not possible that Abraham had felt "threatened by some dire calamity to his tribe or frantic because of some fatal epidemy. . . . Some harrowing emergency may have brought the thought of this supreme and ultimate sacrifice of the ancient world."[4] Some descriptions or characterizations —for instance of the scene between the father and his son who wants to know where the lamb for the sacrifice is—lead a commentator to the threshold of exaggeration or of a false sentimentality. John Skinner says for instance: "The pathos of this dialogue is inimitable, the artless curiosity of the child, the irrepressible affection of the father, and the stern ambiguity of his reply can hardly be read without tears."[3]

To quote a Jewish commentator, Julian Morgenstern, the sacrifice story is "recognized as one of the classics of world-literature." Its author's art is incomparable. Apart from its surpassing artistic merit the narrative is "because of the spiritual lesson it conveys sublime and inspiring to the highest degree. Hardly any other story in the Bible equals and certainly none does surpass it."[5]

In discussing the wreath of legends which the rabbis bound around that jewel-story, we have already mentioned that some of the commentaries resulted in paraphrases or obtained the character of explanation of the narrative. In the Mishnah it is for instance remarked that Abraham had many temptations and that the greatest of them was the demand of the Lord to sacrifice Isaac.

Here emerges, of course, the traditional exegesis asserting that the event is theologically viewed as the supreme trial and triumph of Abraham's faith. Compared with the significance of the sacrifice for the first patriarch in this exegesis, its importance for Isaac is scarcely considered. Since this problem will occupy our attention in another context, we postpone its discussion.

It should only be mentioned that allusions to some early legendary features appear in the hair-splitting discussions of rabbis even at the much later Talmudic phase. Here, for instance, is a sample of such an allusion during a discussion. The rabbis pondered the question of whether the Lord would unite His sacred name with that of men. He would do this only after their death, since the inclination to evil may prevail over them while they are alive. Yet, thus runs the counter-argument, God united His name with that of Isaac since He said to Jacob "I am the God of thy father Isaac." "Why was this?" asked the rabbis. The answer is that God counted Isaac's willingness to die on the altar as though he had actually died for His sake.[6] Even in this diluted form, which equates an emotional potentiality with real death, the old tradition of Isaac's "first death" in the fire and of his resurrection re-emerges.

It is certainly of some psychological interest that the trial of Abraham (called Ibrahim in Arabic) also plays a role in the Koran. Its Sura XXXVII concerns itself with this Biblical theme. Some theologians assert that not Isaac, but his brother Ishmael, the progenitor of Mohammed, was the subject of the arrested sacrifice. On the sacrificial feast Id-a-adha the story of Ishmael's sacrifice is commemorated in a prayer praising the goodness of Allah.

Here we could discuss the commentaries of rabbis and church fathers dealing with the redemptive functions of Isaac's near sacrifice. If this narrative is comparable to a bunch of wild flowers, many of the commentaries have rather the dryness or lifelessness of flowers in a herbarium. In such commentaries fantastic or even artificial plants are not entirely absent. Eduard Stucken's astrological explanation,[7] Hugo Winckler's interpretations of Abraham and Isaac as representing forms of the moon-god,[8] Ignaz Goldziher's concept[9] of Abraham as the heaven at night, of Sarah as the moon and of Isaac as the sun, show a more luxuriant imagination than many fairy tales. But our attention is still held by the attempts of modern scholars to explain the Genesis story.

The following samples from modern exegesis of the Genesis narrative are taken at random. Completeness is neither aspired to nor attainable. An admittedly cursory study of interpretations of the tale leads to the impression that the majority of commentators agree about two fundamental points: first that the narrative means to show that Yahweh rejects human sacrifice, and secondly that the story glorifies the patriarch in demonstrating Abraham's wonderful faith as it is proved in his terrible test.

To quote the recent commentary by Julian Morgenstern before mentioned: It is pointed out that, historically seen, the story "was designed to combat what was in the 9th, 8th, and 7th centuries B.C. an overgrowing evil, the horrible practice of child sacrifice." There is, of course, another purpose served by it: it should show that even the richest animal sacrifice is less valuable than unconditional love of God, than the sacrifice of the heart.

This is essentially the tenor of most modern interpretations of the Genesis chapter, however differently they otherwise deal with the persons and situations presented in this part of the Scripture. According to the *Interpreter's Bible*[10] the chapter has to be read "with discretion and discrimination" because in it are truths before which one will stand with reverence, and vestiges of old, obsolete ideas.

How did this horrible story of human sacrifice get into the Bible? It was desired to show that Abraham's devotion to the Lord he worshiped was capable of going to the farthest point that religion could reach. Abraham saw that the Canaanite tribes were offering their children to their gods. The commentators continue here in presenting a "psychological" theory: in spite of the torment in his soul the patriarch could not help hearing an inward voice asking him why "he should not do as much." He conceived of that admonition pressing upon his conscience as the voice of God.

Surprisingly enough, the voice of God says ultimately something completely different: it is not the sacrifice of Isaac that God demands, but love and mercy "and the knowledge of God more than burnt offerings" (Hosea VI: 6). The Almighty reveals Himself not as a cruel Moloch, but as our father.

At this point the question emerges: how can two facts that seem contradictory be brought into unity? God prevents the sacrifice of Isaac while Abraham is ready to perform it. There is "a sovereign loyalty" which overlooks the ordinary reservations of affection. Also, these commentators come to the final conclusion that the intent of the narrative was to explain why human sacrifice was no longer offered at the sanctuary and that this kind of devotion had no place in the worship of Israel's God.

To Lawther Clarke, a recent commentator, the obvious background of the narrative is the deepened religious sentiment of Israel as a result of the prophetic teaching which made it impossible "to come to terms with the human sacrifices practiced by the surrounding nations."[11] This author asserts that the story must be comparatively late. He draws this conclusion from the fact that the angel of Yahweh (probably a substitute for Yahweh Himself) speaks at a distance from Heaven.

Benno Jacob[12] begins his interpretation with the declaration "if one wants to psychologize" and applies his "psychological" insight especially to the interpretation of the last scene of the drama in which the patriarch does not carry out what he intended to do. In the case that one wants to "psychologize," this author asserts, one has to assume that that call from Heaven staying Abraham's hand came really from the deepest ground of his heart in the last moment. The process in him could perhaps be expressed in the words: "No, I cannot want that!" The knife in Abraham's raised hand brings about the sudden turn: pointed at a person, even at one's own child—this cannot be the sacrifice God demands. "It would be murder."

This and other interpretations of the story are all in a major key. Otto Proksch, for instance, points out [13] that it is the same God demanding Isaac's sacrifice and redeeming him, but the recognition of this god is different before and after. Before the scene on the mountain, God was conceived as a mysterious power removing Abraham from his parental home and then asking him to sacrifice the son promised to him. Afterwards those cruel features of God have vanished. His mercy emerges and remains

His fundamental characteristic in the patriarchal time. With the end of the sacrifice scene we enter a new phase of the history of religion, and Abraham is conceived as the conqueror of the practice of human sacrifice in the Hebrew religion.

I think these examples of theological and exegetic interpretations are enough. We may now break off this sketchy survey and turn to another kind of explanation.

CHAPTER IV

The Anthropological and Archaeological Approach

I MPORTANT DISCOVERIES due to archaeological excava-
tions, as well as progress made in the area of philology
and comparative religion, have helped us considerably to understand certain myths and concepts of the
ancient Near East. There is, however, a tendency to ex-

THE CHALLENGE OF THE PROBLEM

aggerate the importance of the insights obtained by recent archaeological findings, as if they could prove the truth or the historicity of the Bible. The so-called "confirmations" of the patriarchal story prove that the Genesis narratives are true to the facts of nomadic life, but nothing else. Only a very superficial view can see in them confirmations of the historic truth of those Biblical tales.

The progress of archaeology and anthropology cast some light on the customs and religious nature of the ancestors of the Israelites, but none on their individual lives. A Viennese writer said of a certain lady who could talk glibly of Shakespeare's plays and Rembrandt's pictures: "Yes; her ignorance has some astonishing gaps." Recent archaelogical discoveries highlight the fact that our ignorance of Hebrew origins has similarly wide lacunae.

In certain ways the anthropological and achaeological approach to the interpretation of our Genesis story is close to the exegetical attempts at explanation. Both take their point of departure from the central theme of human sacrifice and try to understand the Biblical narrative in terms of this primitive practice. Anthropologists and historians who compare the Genesis tradition with their own material point out that sacrifices of children were widely practiced among the people of the ancient Near

: 46 :

East. They refer to many passages of contemporary writers to prove the existence of this custom.

Plutarch describes vividly how the Carthaginians slew children as "if they were lambs or chickens" [1] on the altar of their god Moloch, and the Egyptian mothers threw their children to the holy crocodiles of the Nile.[2] The children of the Phoenicians were brought as sacrifices to Baal.[3] The Second Book of Kings reports that when the King of Moab saw that the battle threatened to be in his disfavor "he took his oldest son that should have reigned in his stead, and offered him as a burnt offering upon the wall." (II Kings III: 26, 27). The Canaanites, who were akin to the Hebrews, likewise offered their children to the gods.

Deuteronomy emphatically warns the Israelites against following the model of the neighboring people: "Thou shalt not do so unto the Lord thy god: for every abomination to the Lord, which he hateth, have they done unto their gods; for even their sons and daughters they have burnt in the fire to their gods." (Deut. XII: 31) The prophet Micah, who fought desperately against Israel's relapse into paganism during the reigns of Jotham, Ahaz and Hezekiah, challenged the custom of sacrifice:

> Shall I give my firstborn for my transgression,
> The fruit of my body for the sin of my soul?
> (Micah VI: 7)

: 47 :

The Israelites made burnt offering of their children to Baal or Moloch at a place called Tophet. It was situated in the sinister valley of Hinnom, outside the walls of Jerusalem. In the seventh century, as we read in the Second Book of Kings, Ahaz "made his son to pass through the fire" (II Kings XVI: 3) and King Manasseh did likewise. Deuteronomy expressed intensive horror at these customs and compared them with the worst acts of idolatry: "There shall not be found among you any one that maketh his son or his daughter to pass through the fire, or that useth divination, or an observer of times, or an enchanter, or a witch, or a charmer, or a consulter with familiar spirits, or a wizard, or a necromancer. For all that do these things are an abomination unto the Lord: and because of these things abominations the Lord thy God doth drive them out from before thee." (Deut. XVIII: 10-12).

Ezekiel compared the slaughter of children with idolatry and whoring on high places and was horrified by them: "For when ye offer your gifts, when you make your sons to pass through the fire, ye pollute yourselves . . ." (Ezek. XVI: 20-26; XX: 31)

All the prophets attacked that pagan custom. Jeremiah fought with all his power against the horrible events of Tophet. "And they have built the high places of Tophet . . . to burn their sons and their daughters in the fire.

... Therefore, behold, the days come, saith the Lord, that it shall no more be called Tophet, nor the valley of the son of Hinnom, but the valley of slaughter: for they shall bury in Tophet, till there be no place. And the carcasses of this people shall be meat for the fowls of the heaven, and for the beasts of the earth; and none shall fray them away. Then I will cause to cease from the cities of Judah, and from the streets of Jerusalem, the voice of mirth, and the voice of gladness, the voice of the bridegroom, and the voice of the bride: for the land will be desolate" (Jer. VII: 31-34. See also Jer. XIX: 5-15).

Scholars have shown that the legends of other ancient people report sacrifices of children similar to the one recounted in the Genesis story. As early as 1907 Eduard Stucken turned our attention to the parallel between the Isaac and the Oedipus saga: like Isaac, Oedipus was nearly killed by his father and, like Isaac, the Theban hero became blind later on. The legend of the sacrifice of Iphigenia, King Agamemnon's daughter, to Artemis and the story of Jephta's daughter, vowed and sacrificed to Yahweh, were often compared with the Genesis tradition.

The content of the Genesis saga leaves no doubt that it expresses the idea that the original sacrifice of the son among the Hebrews was replaced by the sacrifice of an animal. The question, at which phase of the development of Hebrew religion this substitution took place, remains. Was it really at the age of Abraham as the Genesis tradition reports?

Asking this question immediately raises another one, namely that of the historicity of the patriarch. It is perhaps appropriate to discuss this problem at this point. It has a history itself since it is connected with the change of our views about the prehistoric past of Israel. Here is a short outline of these changes.

There were three definite theories about the Biblical figures of Abraham, Isaac and Joseph. The first, represented by Stucken, Hugo Winckler and Eduard Meyer, sees Abraham, Isaac and Joseph as original astral deities, mostly as different forms of the moon god. Winckler founded his theory on analogies with the mythology of the Babylonians. This scholar asserts that all that is reported of Isaac is merely a repetition of the Abraham legends.[4] He points to the Genesis narrative in which Isaac in Gerar pretends that his wife is his sister as Abraham had before him (Gen. XII: 11-13), to the Abimelech episode as a diluted repetition, and to the tale of the well as also mirrored in Isaac's story. Isaac is in his view a feeble Yahwistic copy ("Abklatsch") of the figure of Abraham.

In contrast with him Eduard Meyer[5] is more inclined to identify the patriarchs with local deities of Canaan: for instance Abraham with the four gods who are at home in Hebron, and Isaac with the local god of Beer-sheba. For those interpreters as well as for Eduard Stucken, Ignaz Goldziher and others, the sky is not the limit, but it is the appropriate home of the patriarchs who were originally astral deities.

Another theory declares that the figures of Abraham, Isaac and Joseph do not represent individual persons, but clans and tribes. Lewis Heyward (in the *New Standard Bible Dictionary*)[6] assumes that probably under the name of Abraham are preserved traditions of great tribal movements which began in Arabia, followed the Euphrates, crossed to Haran and ended by penetrating Canaan. Driver, on the other hand, thinks that the view "best to satisfy the circumstances of the case" is that Abraham, Isaac and Joseph are "historical persons, and that the accounts which we have of them are in outline historically true."[7]

An eminent orientalist, E. O. James, recently pointed out that Abraham might have been a historic character but that in the Genesis narratives "an ethnological motif predominated and tribal relationships and rivalries have been presented in terms of individual adventures of eponymous ancestors of Israel." The narratives might contain historical elements in relation to tribal conditions, occasionally even to actual persons, but, James continues, "they are historical only in the sense of being the record of certain significant episodes in the life of the nation long after they have taken place." They are not, of course, contemporary records; an interval of a thousand or fifteen hundred years separates them from the actual events described.

Each story has its own independent existence and was drawn up for its particular purpose, ethnological or religious. To discover the point of significance in the composite narrative as in the whole, each story has to be examined and evaluated as a separate entity detached from the general traditions in their final form.[8] That is a good suggestion to follow also when we examine the Isaac story.

Biblical scholars are nowadays more and more inclined to believe in the historicity of Abraham, Isaac and Jacob. Salo Wittmayer Baron for instance points to the "lifelike descriptions of the human strengths and weaknesses of the patriarchs which reflect probably historic persons."[9] O. Jeremias considers it no longer "a matter of argument that behind the Biblical Abraham an important personality is manifest, a prophetic leader equal in stature to Mohammed."[10] In contrast to such an evaluation Yehezkel Kaufman states in his recent scholarly work *History of the Religion of Israel*[11] that the Bible itself attests indirectly to the fact that Israel's monotheism is post-patriarchal. There is no reference to a battle with idolatry or to a

religious conflict between the patriarchs and their sur-
roundings. Later legends seized upon Abraham, making
him the father of the Israelite religion.

Even Sir Leonard Woolly, who is inclined to assume the
historicity of Abraham, has admitted that there is no
direct evidence for it in non-Biblical documents while
indirect evidence is "possible." He considers it to be not
a coincidence that the ram caught in a thicket and slain
in Isaac's stead recalls a figure stereotyped in Sumerian
art.[12] Harold H. Rowley recently stated that it is "quite
misleading to suggest that archaeology proves the truth
of the Bible." None of the patriarchs is mentioned outside the Scriptures and no incident in which "they fig-
ured is recorded in any contemporary source."[13]

We have omitted a number of more recent contributions to the problem of the historicity of Abraham and
Isaac. Most of the authors of these investigations are
strictly noncommittal. A random thought compares their
attitude with that seen in a recent photograph of the actor
and writer Peter Ustinov performing a comical parody
of a British diplomat. His gestures in delivering his
speech are elucidated by the caption: "Her Majesty's
Government, while not saying nay to the motion, yet
does not say aye. This should in no way be construed
as an abstention."[14]

To become serious again: There is not the slightest

direct evidence for the historicity of Abraham. The indirect evidence taken from inscriptions and other archaeological findings is not at all sufficient to prove his existence. The solution to this question, however, is not essential to the progress of our inquiry, which is directed to the restoration of the original oral tradition underlying the Genesis story of Isaac's near sacrifice.

I would like, however, to make an observation that might be relevant to our exploration. It seems to me that the two modern theories here presented are not irreconcilable. Even if Abraham should eventually be recognized as a historical personality (which I doubt), it might well be possible that he was later on identified with certain clans or tribes. To compare the situation with another one: Let us assume for a moment that new archaeological discoveries make it certain that the patriarch Jacob was an actual person living at a certain time at the court of a pharaoh. Does this certainty exclude the possibility that a people were called by Jacob's later name, Israel (Gen. XXXII: 28)?

Or to take an example closer to our time: Let us assume that new findings disclose beyond doubt that Christ's figure is based on historic happenings. Does the fact not remain that millions of people are called Christians? It seems to me that the possibility of Abraham's historicity does not exclude the other possibility that his figure represents certain tribes. It is highly imaginable that the legend of Abraham and Isaac can be traced back to an old tradition in which certain religious practices and tribal customs were identified with forefathers from whom the early Hebrews allegedly descended.

It is very possible that these rites and customs were tied to anonymous chieftains in archaic times, and that later on their origin was attributed to certain cult heroes such as Abraham and Isaac. The comparison with the folklore of Australian and African aborigines shows that tribal tradition frequently connects old customs and institutions to legendary figures of a remote past. What remains is not a mystery, but an obscurity.

CHAPTER V

The Existential Concept of the Myth

ONE DOESN'T GET AROUND difficulties by ignoring them, and great difficulties are met when one reads the Genesis story for the first time. The child who hears the tale of Isaac's sacrifice is father to the man who remembers it and perplexedly ponders it. In the view of the *Interpreter's Bible* the episode of Isaac's sacrifice "may seem incredible or profoundly disturbing to children in Sunday school."[1] The child will object to the contradictions in it and claim that the picture of the Lord depicted here does not correspond to the one painted elsewhere. The little boy or the little girl is not afraid to say that the emperor has no clothes on.

In the prelude to his book *Fear and Trembling,*[2] written in 1843, the Danish philosopher Sören Kierkegaard recounts that he heard that story as a child. As an adult he read it again and with great admiration. The older he became, the more frequently his mind reverted to that story; his enthusiasm became greater and greater, and yet he was less and less able to understand it. He wished then that he might have been able to follow Abraham and Isaac on their journey.

He does not speak here of the horror he must have experienced when he first heard the narrative. But in his book, *Training in Christianity,* published in 1850, he freely confesses that as a child he experienced that shock which most people feel when they make their first acquaintance with the adventure of Abraham and Isaac on Mount Moriah. It seems that Kierkegaard's religious belief almost foundered at that time.

In his Journal he uses the lines from *Faust:*

> Half childplay
> Half God in the heart

as a motto when he tells us that he felt as horrified as other children who, after being delighted with pictures of William Tell and Napoleon, see the picture of Christ's suffering and death for the first time. An echo of that early shock will be perceived by any reader of *Fear and Trembling,* in Kierkegaard's dramatic description of Abraham and Isaac walking together to the place for the sacrifice.

It is as if the writer had realized his old wish to accompany them on their fateful journey. Kierkegaard intensified the horror in imagining the last phase of the journey: Abraham has now to tell his son that God demanded his death. Isaac falls at his father's knee and begs for his young life. Abraham turns around for a moment but when Isaac sees his face again it is changed. His glance is ferocious; he seizes Isaac by the throat, throws him to the ground and shouts, "Stupid boy, did you suppose that I am thy father? I worship idols. Do you suppose that it is God's demand? No, it is my desire." Isaac trembles and crying out in terror pleads with the Lord to have compassion with him, but Abraham thanks God because it is better for Isaac to believe that his father is a monster than to lose faith in the Creator.

The philosopher and thinker Kierkegaard elaborates from this point to the theme of faith in far-reaching reflections, until he arrives at the conclusion which he calls the paradox in the case of Abraham. The dread "which can well make a man sleepless" consists in a contradiction. The ethical expression for the deed of the patriarch is that he would murder his son for religious reasons. When faith is removed "there only remains the crude fact that Abraham wanted to murder Isaac." Kierkegaard is not afraid to recognize "the verdict of truth that Abraham was a murderer."

In the part of his book entitled Problem Two, Kierkegaard asks, "Is there such a thing as an absolute duty toward God?" The next part (Problem Three) formulates and discusses the question: "Was Abraham ethically defensible in keeping silent about his purpose before Sarah, before Eleazar, before Isaac?" The enormous paradox Kierkegaard confronts us with is this: Either the individual as individual is able to stand in an absolute relation to the absolute, or Abraham is lost. The patriarch cannot speak, because what he would have to convey is unsayable. Therefore his distress and his anguish. He cannot say that it is a test, and a test of such a kind that it is simultaneously a temptation.

If he spoke to Isaac, he would transform the situation into the temptation. (Kierkegaard uses here the German word *Anfechtung*.) With his idea of the paradox in Abraham's case, the Dane stands with all exegesists of his time who depart from a preconceived idea of religious faith and of the test to which Abraham is subjected, yet see him as the "father of faith." The patriarch's faith is made possible only through the suspension of the ethical. In truth the requirements of ethics and the requirements of faith conflict here. Is Abraham a potential murderer, or only an obedient servant of his God? The problem cannot be settled until after the test. Abraham does not reject the ethical. He goes beyond it.

There is no need to enter into a discussion of Kierkegaard's "paradoxical religiosity" at this point. The intensity of emotion with which his writings are charged proves that he unconsciously identified with Isaac. It may be helpful to call to mind a fact emphasized by the biographers of the Danish philosopher: his father considered his youngest son Sören not only as his Benjamin, but also "as his Isaac, the son who is to be sacrificed as his atonement, or, at least for his guilt."[3] The "crazy" educational devices of this father, who was doubtlessly an emotionally deeply disturbed man, left lasting impressions on the perceptive son and determined the character of his views about Abraham and Isaac, whose story he morbidly pondered. The Abraham parable forms the main theme of his book *Fear and Trembling* and quite a few of his followers often refer to it to illustrate their philosophical or theological thesis.

This is not the place to pursue the influence of Kierkegaard upon Karl Barth and his dialectical or "crisis" theology, nor upon the views of Emil Brunner, Martin Buber, Reinhold Niebuhr, Martin Heidegger, Karl Jaspers and others who marched farther along the side-path the Dane first trod. They occasionally refer to the Biblical problem with which he had to grapple. Jean-Paul Sartre still discusses that *"angoisse d'Abraham"* and is immersed in it: All is well if it is really an angel who comes and says: "Thou art Abraham and thou shalt sacrifice thy son!" But, Sartre continues, everybody may ask himself if it is an angel and if I am Abraham. Who can prove that that voice came from heaven and not from hell or from the unconscious or from a pathological state?[4]

Kierkegaard's existential interpretation of the Genesis narrative influenced not only the theological circle around Karl Barth, but certain Jewish theologians as well. It also aroused the opposition of some Jewish and philosophical groups. I will mention as an example the lecture given by Ignaz Maybaum at the Leo Baeck College in London. The scholarly author asserts that Kierkegaard's commentary to the Genesis story "presents an impressive spectacle of how a text of the Old Testament transforms itself before the eyes of the reader into a text which could be found in the New Testament."[5] It is conceived in the most consistent Pauline tradition.

Maybaum compares and contrasts the trust Abraham

shows with the faith of St. Paul and Kierkegaard, and in doing this sees a contradiction between Mount Moriah and Golgotha. The prevailing difference between the world of the Old Testament and that of the New lies in the distinction between trust and faith. Kierkegaard describes faith an an "action." Trust is, in contrast to faith, an attitude and has no aim, whereas every action has necessarily its aim. Abraham who trusts does not need to make those "movements upwards" nor "the leap" of which Kierkegaard speaks. The patriarch walks humbly before his God.

In this lecture Maybaum treads the same path as Benjamin Segal had a few decades earlier.[6] He, like his predecessor, comes to the conclusion that there is an insurmountable difference between Abraham's willingness to sacrifice his beloved son and Jesus' death as self-sacrifice.

The existential concept is discussed here only as it deals with the Genesis story of Isaac's sacrifice and Abraham's "collision," to use Kierkegaard's expression. Although Kierkegaard is concerned with the theological aspect of that narrative, existentialism is mainly interested in the psychology of the Biblical figures, in the dramatis personae.

CHAPTER VI

Psychoanalytic
Interpretations

MYTHS ARE the collective daydreams of mankind. They reflect the personal relationships between parents and children, between brothers, between wife and husband, as they appeared as facts and as potentialities to the minds of ancient people. In myths the gods often have the function and place of parents, elevated to divine rank. When you reduce them to their original place, the psychological problems of relationship within the family remain to challenge the explorer who is eager to discover the meaning behind the myth.

As reflected in the sagas of the Bible, "life with father" was not easy for the sons of the patriarch Abraham. Its complexity became an early subject of psychoanalytic investigations. We have seen that prior to them Eduard Stucken had pointed out the similarity between the Oedipus myth and the Biblical Isaac tradition.[1]

In his work on the incest-motif in sagas and literature first published in 1912, Otto Rank conceived of Isaac's sacrifice, prevented only at the last moment, as a threat to castrate Abraham's son. A confirmation of this hypothesis is, he asserts, to be seen in the fact that God made the covenant of circumcision. According to this solemn agreement, all males should be circumcised when eight days old. Circumcision is to be understood as a diluted or mitigated form of castration, displaced, in some myths, to other organs. The piercing of Oedipus' ankle joints is thus a disguised castration by his father Laius.[2]

The most recent psychoanalytic contributions to the problem are published by Dorothy Zeligs, who has made a thorough study of the Abramitic period. In her first paper[3] on this subject she considers the Genesis story a presentation of the ambivalent attitude of Abraham towards his son. As Otto Rank before her, she considers it significant that the "covenant of the pieces which God established with Abraham was effected at the time when the Lord promised that He would grant him and Sarah a son." A partial castration was thus the prize which God exacted for a son whose existence placed Abraham in a position analogous to that of the father-God. When the son achieved an age when he could displace his father —as Abraham took the place of Terah—"hostility and guilt created a crisis with its peak in the near sacrifice of Isaac." This was an act which would have been in the service both of feelings of hostility and the need for punishment. But Abraham's positive feelings, his love for the son, gained the ascendancy, overcoming hostility and guilt.

In his book, *The Meaning of Sacrifice,* Roger E. Money-Kyrle also places the significance of the Isaac story in the Oedipus situation. Unlike Rank and Zeligs, who center their attention on the attitude of the father, the British author considers the scene on Mount Moriah from the psychological point of view of the victim. He too finds the key to the mythical problem in the Oedipus situation, but rather in the unconscious wish of the son to kill and displace the father. In following this track, he concludes that for Isaac "the sacrifice is the realization of the inverted Oedipus fantasy in which the killing is done, not by himself, but by his father and in which he, not his father is the victim."[4]

Isaac's sacrifice would thus amount to a kind of expiatory act and his satisfaction in it would be of a masochistic nature, originating in the fantasy of being killed by Abraham. In identifying with the executioner the victim interprets his slaughter as a punishment from God and gets masochistic gratification in that act in which he atones for his murderous wishes against his father.

In the analytic contributions quoted above, the Genesis saga of Isaac's sacrifice is only a side theme. It is, however, the subject of a book a young psychiatrist, Erich Wellisch, wrote in 1953, entitled *Isaac and Oedipus*.[5] This study is "based on the observation that phenomena which were described in the Bible occur in every person and provide a unique source for psychological research and insight." It is his conviction that "this approach provides the most satisfactory hypothesis for the motivations in parent-child relationships and thus for human conduct in general."[6]

In exploring the Isaac myth, Wellisch's point of view is the reverse of that of his psychoanalytic predecessors. They tried to understand the emotional processes described in the Scriptural stories by the analogy to phenomena observed in everyday life. Wellisch does not see

in the sagas of the Bible a confirmation of those psychological theories, but is convinced "that studies in Biblical
psychology provide a necessary requirement for the
development of psychiatry." Such a conviction becomes
understandable when one hears the author complain that
"the atheistic and pantheistic aspects of modern psychology lead to dangerous conclusions." Wellisch demands that psychology and theology fructify each other
"forming a synthetic science," and predicts that this
future psychology "would accept the reality and the
uniqueness of the God of Biblical religion."[7]

Wellisch's scholarly book starts with a survey of the
custom of ancient and primitive infanticide, its aspects
and motives. It discusses as did its predecessors, the aspects of the Oedipus complex, and then passes to the
main theme, the investigation of the Akedah (the binding of Isaac) experience and its psychological significance. The main thesis is that Abraham resolved his
Oedipus complex by the victory of love over his jealousy
and hostility towards the son.

In discussing analytic concepts Wellisch makes the
critical comment that in the attempts to formulate basic
psychological theories no positive use has so far been
made of Biblical beliefs. He points out that the central
psychoanalytic concept of character and neuroses is
shaped after the Greek Oedipus myth, and expresses his

wish that Biblical motifs should receive more recognition in modern psychological theories.

Here, it seems to me, is a confusion of the content of psychological concepts and their name-giving. When we speak of the Oedipus complex, we apply the name of the Greek myth in which the basic features of a certain emotional constellation are dramatically presented. This is a question of terminology dictated mainly by personal taste (in this case Freud's) and kept for reasons of expediency.

Apropos of personal taste, Wellisch's interpretation is put in pure "Psychoanalese," as I have called the odd jargon of our science. Here are a few samples from Wellisch's book: In the last moment Isaac saw Heaven "because he had overcome his Oedipus complex completely." Abraham on the other hand saw it not, for he still struggled with the last convulsions of his Laius Complex. Sarah, who had let her son go, "conquered her Jocasta Complex." As an aside it is mentioned that the Electra Complex that appears in the experience of the Biblical Ruth is not presented in the Isaac myth.

The combination of Greek and Biblical mythical figures, or rather the application of names from Greek mythology to the patriarchal story, makes a grotesque impression. But the merciless criticism Wellisch's book evokes does not exclude the admission that it contains quite a few thoughtful remarks and at least one new suggestion on which I will comment later on.

The analytic authors I quoted are mainly interested in the figures of Abraham and Isaac from the psychological viewpoint. That means they try to understand the emotional and mental processes in these figures as if they were living persons. The material at their disposal is used to find the psychic dynamics and mechanisms. The Genesis stories are treated as if they were histories, or rather case stories.

Such a treatment is exposed to criticism of two kinds. The first is that the saga material available is too scarce, uncertain, and scanty to allow such a use of psychoanalytic research methods. The second is that the figures of Abraham and Sarah are legendary and their emotions and thoughts cannot be analyzed in the same way as, let me say, those of Mr. John Day and Mrs. Jane Black, nor even of those of Napoleon and his wife Josephine.

Besides and beyond those arguments it has to be said that this kind of analytic demonstration—not to say display—is today obsolete and outdated, if it was ever justified. Comparatively speaking it would be as though American soldiers would go to war in 1961 equipped with Civil War muskets, or as though you would prepare yourself for the solution of a problem of higher mathematics by demonstrating the correctness of the multiplication table.

Instead, therefore, of evaluating the individual psycho-analytic contributions to our problem, I prefer to point out in what way they are different in character and purpose from the study here presented. To define the differences in dealing with the material: the analytic authors whose contributions were discussed here are interested in personalia. They want to discover the unconscious motives and aims of Biblical figures. We want to use the saga material to discover some of the unexplained or unknown social and religious customs of the earliest Hebrew clans, to reconstruct the prehistoric past of Semitic tribes.

CHAPTER VII

On Second Consideration

H AVING DRAWN the distinction between previous
attempts at analytic explanation and our present line of investigation, we can now turn
to second thoughts. Let me first briefly consider how the
theological and exegetic comments, the historical and
archaeological contributions, and the existential interpretations have helped us in our search to understand the
Biblical narrative. We learned much from them all, but
they were unable to lead us to the solution of the problem that challenges us. It is, of course, easy to show that

each of those attempts sheds some light on certain aspects of the problem, but none gives us the key to it.

We will unhesitatingly dismiss the theological approach of fundamentalism that accepts the literal truth of the Genesis story. This view denies, of course, that there is a problem, since it believes the Genesis tradition *"en bloc."* Since we conceive of it as a myth, we are standing on different ground. No bridge leads from scientific investigation to the land of faith. We are separated from the area of faith by the abyss that yawns between research and belief. A similar obstacle exists between our aim and that of the existentialists, who point out that Abraham's problem is essentially a paradox or that his conflict was solved by a "leap"—an expression Kierkegaard uses. No such movement can transport us to a region where faith and not truth is the greatest recognized value.

The aims of the modern Biblical scholars and exegetists are akin to ours and we gratefully acknowledge their help. They too want to find out what was the religious and social situation of ancient Israel. Yet we hesitate to make unrestricted use of many contributions of this kind. Some of the conclusions drawn from the legendary material are ambiguous and few are valid and complete. A majority of Biblical scholars are inclined to assume the historicity of the Genesis figures. Many exegetists not only conceive of Abraham and Isaac as historic figures, but also accept as fact the tradition that Abraham introduced the substitution of animal sacrifice for human sacrifice. In the absence of evidence for a historic Abraham, we can accept the probability that this figure was created in a manner similar to that of a culture hero, as anthropologists call it; that is, as a figure to whom the people of antiquity and primitive tribes of our time attribute some technical or cultural innovation such as the substitution of animal offering for human sacrifice.

But even granting the possible historicity of Abraham, nothing is known from extra-Biblical sources of the existence of his two sons, Ishmael and Isaac. We remind the reader of the observation of Hugo Winckler who asserted that the Isaac story is only a diluted copy of the Abraham legend. There are enough conspicuous elements in the Genesis tradition to indicate that the original saga material was fragmented and applied to two figures, or that the same tradition appeared in two versions. We know that similar apportionments appeared in phenomena psychologically akin to myth formation, namely in dreams and neurotic symptoms. Ludwig Jekels has demonstrated in valuable papers that certain emotional factors are responsible for such overlapping expressions of psychic themes.[1]

Even a historian like Carl Heinrich Cornill, who believes that Abraham was a historic personage, is not ready to attribute the same character to the descendants of the patriarch. He admits that "it might be thought that what is true of the father should be true for his sons and grandchildren," but such a conclusion could be considered premature. Cornill presents a good example of muddled thinking of such a kind: "Greek tradition ascribes to Lycurgus, the lawgiver of Sparta, two sons, Eunomos and Encosmos, i.e. Law and Order." No reasonable person will doubt that Lycurgus was "an historical personage, but that he actually had had two sons, named 'Law' and 'Order' will scarcely be believed." The historian points out that the names which the tradition gives to patriarchal figures are all names of races and tribes and we are here "beyond question in the realm of personification." Tribes never adopt the names of individuals, but the patronymic tribal ancestor comes first and then becomes a composite or personification of the people. However plastic and distinct the individualities of Ishmael or Isaac may seem to be, they are only representations or personifications of the races or tribes whose name they bear. The scholar sees an indication of this fact—he calls it "a glimmer of this truth"—in the tradition that Rebecca before the birth of her twins received the divine announcement:

Two nations are in thy womb
And two people shall be separated even from thy bowels

And the one people shall be stronger than the other people
And the elder shall serve the younger.

Other scholars also are of the opinion that the name of
Isaac was probably originally that of a tribe. It could be
understood as "God laughs," either as an expression of
grace towards the man or as one of scorn toward the
tribe's enemies. It has also to be considered that Isaac's
picture in the Scriptures is rather colorless. He has no
heroic traits of character. The second of the patriarchs
resembles Abraham, but he has "less significance in the
Biblical account than either his father or his son."[2] Isaac
has no strongly marked personal features. What dis-
tinguishes him from other Biblical figures are not sharply
defined traits, but certain situations in which we find
him. We are less interested in his personality than in his
vicissitudes.

The most meaningful of those situations is certainly
that described as his near sacrifice, in which he appears
almost entirely as a passive figure, as an obedient victim.
How does this very scene appear in the evaluation of the
Biblical scholars and exegetists? Modern research workers
almost unanimously consider the Genesis narrative as
an etiological myth—as a saga that explains how it came
about that the people of Israel did not sacrifice human
beings any longer, but used animals instead. The content
of that scene leaves no doubt that Abraham wanted to

bring his beloved son as a burnt offering to the Lord, who stayed his knife in the last moment. The premise unexpressed is, of course, that the Hebrews in older days offered their children to their god as sacrifice.[3]

As we indicated in Chapter IV, the books and papers of historians and exegetists contain abundant anthropological material about the practice of infanticide among the ancient people, especially among the illiterate tribes of Australia and Africa. Biblical passages bear witness to the historical fact that the custom was also observed by the Hebrews at a certain time of their history. Archaeological findings confirm the assumption that at a certain definable age child sacrifice was established in Palestine.

It is not correct to assume that human sacrifice is a practice characteristic of primitive society. We find, on the contrary, that the practice of infanticide and human sacrifice can appear "when a relatively high culture had developed."[4] The Aztecs did not adopt the practice until the fourteenth century. The people of the Eastern Mediterranean, such as the Carthaginians, the Canaanites and the Phoenicians, who sacrificed their children to their god, were on a much higher cultural level than the still-nomadic Hebrew clans at the supposed time of Abraham. Historians agree that "if tradition is any guide, human sacrifice seems in many important areas to be of secondary character." On the whole, human sacrifice is far commoner among the semi-civilized and barbarous races than in still lower stages of culture.[5]

Yehezkel Kaufman emphasizes in his scholarly work on the religion of Israel that child sacrifice was not practiced except under foreign influence during the reigns of Ahaz and Manasseh.[6] The Elohist story of Isaac's sacrifice was edited and written in final form about 750 B.C. and combined with the Yahwistic source perhaps about 730 B.C., a period in which the sacrifice of children was practiced by the Israelites. Also, in the view of E. O. James, the story of the offering of Isaac is "probably an eighth century prophetic Midrash,"[7] and is in accordance with the Deuteronomic legislation in which the sacrifice of the first-born of man is condemned as an abomination of the surrounding Semitic tribes.

So much for the chronological data. What is the picture which now unfolds? To the clans of early Aramaeans who roamed the grasslands between the fertile area and the desert in search of pasture, human sacrifice was unknown. A least a thousand years separated the nomadic Hebrews whom Abraham led from Mesopotamia into Canaan, from their descendants who made burnt offerings of their children during the reigns of Ahaz and Manasseh in the seventh century.

What are the reasonable conclusions we reach when we consider that the Genesis tale tries to explain that

Abraham substituted a ram for Isaac and that human sacrifice was an abomination to the Lord? The compilers of the Biblical legends—in our case the Elohists—projected the abolishment of human sacrifice upon the past, upon the time of the Hebrew ancestor Abraham who was regarded not only as the father of the nation, but also as a kind of tutelary deity.[8] The Genesis story thus reflects the attitude of certain contemporaries of the prophets, who passionately attacked the recent introduction of child sacrifice which the Israelites had adopted from their neighbors. In short, the sacrifice of children to Yahweh is not a rationalization of the patriarchal period, but an aberration of the time of the late Israelite Kings. The Biblical account is a counterfeit portrait of the patriarch. It is, so to speak, a very clever copy of an old master, but it is not the original.

There are, for instance, several revealing features: The ambiguous image of the deity who has, so to speak, a dual countenance, who is both cruel and merciful. Such a view does not tally with that of a primitive God. There is, furthermore, the idea that God wanted to test Abraham. This is not at all in character with the religious ideas of half-nomadic Bedouin-like tribes in search of pasture. It indicates rather a progressed phase of religious evolution and breathes the atmosphere of the age in which the Book of Job was written, an atmosphere which is post-exilic. There is, so to speak, a fake antiquity in the description of the sacrifice story in that Genesis chapter.

About one hundred and fifty years ago the Russian Otto von Kotzebue observed that the Sandwich Islanders "sacrifice culprits to their gods as we sacrifice them to justice."[9] This remark suggests another comparison by which the character of the Biblical story of Isaac's near sacrifice may be made clear. Let us assume that a lawyer of our time would insert a historic argument into his memoir, in which he pleads for the abolishment of capital punishment. He would, for instance, report that American pioneers had replaced the custom of hanging horse thieves with other measures for the protection of society.

To illustrate the method of quite a few Biblical scholars and historians who try to interpret the Isaac myth, let us assume that an archaeologist about three thousand years after our time finds indubitable proof that in this country certain men were on occasion brought to Sing-Sing and there electrocuted. The archaeologist, furthermore, unearths ancient inscriptions establishing the fact that at a certain phase of history of the now extinct American tribes, this custom was abolished and replaced by a kind of psychiatric or re-educational treatment. The historians who discuss this archaeological discovery would be mistaken if they were to conclude from the existence of capital punishment alone that the American people were at this time on a very low cultural level (although capital punishment is in my view barbarous).

No doubt the historians would now reconstruct a phase in which the prehistoric American people periodically brought human sacrifices to a god they called Justice. Records discovered by the archaeologists would show that the practice of periodical human sacrifice, offered in Sing-Sing, was abolished by a cult-hero who was called President of the United States and had a certain name in the inscriptions deciphered, let us say John Kennedy.

No matter how you twist and turn the features of the Genesis narrative, it cannot be used as a document testifying to the practice of child sacrifice at the age of the early nomadic Hebrew clans. Yet it cannot be fully explained when you conceive of it as a saga composed in the eighth century. When you do not have the key, it does not matter on which side the door is locked.

The Biblical story depicting Abraham's intention to sacrifice his son is, if you want, an etiological myth and explains how it came to pass that the Lord demanded that the original human sacrifice be replaced by animal sacrifice. This is the story, but is it the whole story? When it reveals that the patriarch was the first who put a ram in the place of his son on the altar, does it not also conceal something? Is there not another picture beneath the one describing the scene on Mount Moriah, a much older painting covered by a more recent work and whose traces are still faintly visible when you stand and look at it from certain points?

Almost all commentators and Biblical scholars bring the Isaac story into intimate connection with the practice of human sacrifice by people of ancient times. Hardly one of the interpreters fails to tie it to that rite of the Eastern Mediterranean nations, and almost every one of them points to the analogous myths of Iphigenia sacrificed to Artemis and of Jephta's daughter sacrificed to Yahweh. Yet almost none of them consider that those myths do not belong to a phase of the earliest prehistory, but to a late stage of religious development.

It is as if the whole problem posed by the Genesis tale were solved by the contention that it wants to explain the substitution of animal sacrifice for human sacrifice. Yet this theory certainly does not answer the many questions raised by the Biblical account. The assertion that this is a satisfactory explanation of the Genesis story and its significance is contradicted by the time in which the Isaac incident supposedly takes place as well as by other features. It is too good to be true and too glib to fit into the age of the nomadic patriarchs. The problems of the

Biblical myth are not conquered by that theory of higher criticism and archaeology; they are only circumvented. God who first demands the sacrifice of Isaac and then stays Abraham's knife, still appears in both situations as a *deus ex machina*. The very demand for that sacrifice would cry to heaven if it had not been called down from there.

PART TWO

THE SEARCH
FOR A
SOLUTION

I SHALL LIGHT *a candle of understanding in your heart which shall not be put out.*

II, ESDRAS

CHAPTER VIII

Smoke Screen Around a
Burnt Offering

S EEN FROM A LITERARY VIEWPOINT, the twenty-second
chapter of Genesis is comparable to a short story.
Unlike the novel, a short story isolates and arrests,
presents moments of illusion or disillusion, opens up some
potentiality of character or of destiny. In contrast to the
large structure of the novel the short story, in the words of
a reviewer (Richard Gilman), opens "a shaft drilled very

: 87 :

narrowly into the richest lore in order to come up with exemplary undetailed truth." The Genesis report of Isaac's burnt offering certainly fulfills these requirements.

A well-known novelist, Mary Ellen Chase, recently remarked that there are many empty spaces in the Old Testament, "uncompleted designs and patterns, which arouse curiosity and wonder in our mind. Nowhere are they better illustrated than in the account of Isaac's sacrifice. The power of the story lies in its omissions, in what is not said, in its terrible silence and desolation."[1] Neither Abraham nor Isaac expresses his emotions. In its bareness the story "means more than it can say."[1] The writer compares the tale with the scattered stones of a once carefully wrought building now in ruins. "The stones stand about in the grass with wide spaces between them, each once a part of a whole, yet each more full of meaning in its very solitude."[1] Some people might want to reconstruct the building, "but many of us will not wish to do so, seeing in the single stones an indefinable charm, nameless and ageless."[1]

To remain within the simile: we belong to the people who would like to attempt a reconstruction of the building, especially since we have a hunch that in those empty spaces were once the essential parts of the now half-destroyed ancient house or temple.

We approached the task of reconstruction in the hope

that the exploration of certain features of the Genesis account would give us some insight into the origins of the ancient Hebrews. We hoped that our investigation would perhaps even allow us a glimpse into pre-Abrahamic times. This hope was utterly disappointed. The story that promised to open an approach to a better understanding of prehistoric Israel has all the earmarks of primitivity. Yet we arrived at the conclusion that it is not archaic, but has a younger character. It attributes a custom of the seventh century B.C. to the time of the patriarchs. Here is not a new avenue, here is only a blind alley.

The French language contains the expression *fausse fenêtre,* which means false or fake window. You would use the term for imitations of windows, for instance in the stage set of a theater or for certain architectural designs. They are viewless. That means that you cannot look through them. We now understand that the traditional explanation of the Isaac story presents such a *fausse fenêtre.* We failed to penetrate the secret of the Biblical tale because we took the account of Isaac's near offering at face value and connected it with the practice of human sacrifice observed by the Hebrews as well as by the neighboring people.

We accepted without doubting the literal version of the account instead of asking ourselves what is not said there. We looked at the façade of the tale instead of searching for the inside story. In taking as our point of departure the practice of human sacrifice we started out the wrong way. We relied on the unexamined premise that the Isaac incident posed only the problem of infanticide or sacrifice of the son. It is as if we had attempted to decipher an ancient inscription with a wrong key. We can possibly read some meaning in it, but is it the correct one?

We might feel discouraged and tempted to break off the quest at a point where the Biblical story threatens to become meaningless or rather to have no other meaning than the one demonstrated by the traditional explanation. Is the tale of Isaac's prevented sacrifice a "just-so story"? Is time and effort spent on its exploration wasted?

Let me anticipate that we will discover traces of an older tradition on the very spot where we searched (or near it)—vestiges of forgotten rites, loosely associated with the practice of human sacrifice. Those neglected yet still recognizable features announce themselves by faint signals similar to those perceived by miners deep down in a gallery. It first appears to be impossible to unearth that unknown lost tradition, sunk into oblivion, or to work our way to that invisible subterranean source. But it is not impossible; it is merely very difficult.

What follows is an adventure in psychoanalytic discovery. It would perhaps be advantageous to follow carefully all the steps leading to the discovery; that means the thought-associations from their point of departure in the study of the Biblical material to the point of arrival at a surprising idea. This would, however, lead us too far away, and since the method and purpose of this book claim to be scientific, it might give too subjective a character to the investigation. I cannot avoid, however, sketching, at least in the beginning, the thought-associations that determined the direction of the following exploration. I will pursue them as connecting links from the point where a hunch led slowly to certain assumptions (which were examined) to the point where inspired guesswork led to a growing conviction.

In contrast with my hasty summary of the comments and exegetic attempts to interpret the Isaac myth, the following paragraphs will be an unhurried presentation of the assumptions and of the conclusions reached. Tennyson wrote: "Science moves but slowly, slowly creeping from point to point." Let me preface this demonstration by saying that an investigation such as the one presented here can hardly be undertaken without what L. J. Henderson used to call "an intuitive feel for one's material."

Much sobered by the failure to find a key to the Isaac story, I studied the Biblical account as well as the post-Biblical legends again and found that a nagging thought had quietly slipped into my mind. I paid some attention

to the place in which the Genesis story appears in the Old
Testament, to its context within the Biblical records of the
life of the patriarchs. The Genesis chapter following the
near sacrifice reports Sarah's death and Abraham's pur-
chase of Machpelah where she is buried. But immediately
afterwards the patriarch commissions his old servant to
seek a wife for Isaac among the daughters of Mesopotamia.
It is as if the sacrifice scene were a prelude to this venture
into marriage and as if the future wife, Rebecca, were a
substitute for the beloved mother who had passed away.
Is the place in which the Moriah scene appears accidental?
Has the sequence of events in Isaac's life a meaning? Here,
it seemed to me, is one of those gaps about which Mary
Ellen Chase speaks. Or rather here is the entrance into a
shaft leading into subterranean territory.

Rereading the Biblical account, I was again astonished by
the character of the deity. The God who "did tempt Abraham" is the same God who subjects Job, the man from
Uz, to the supreme test. He is not a deity who talks to the
wandering Bedouin-sheik Abraham as a man talks to his
friend. The God who demands the sacrifice of the only,
beloved son is not identical with the Lord who speaks on
Mount Sinai. The deity in the Isaac story is called Elohim,
but he is a demon. The God painted in this legend cor-
responds as little to the image of the Lord as He appears
in the major part of the Pentateuch, as the man Abraham

does to the picture in the other accounts of the first book of the Scriptures.

The reason for the sacrifice as it is given in the text—namely that the Lord wanted to tempt the patriarch—is obviously a secondary one, what we call a rationalization, a far-fetched explanation covering another, original feature. Here is the God of primitive nomadic clans, who subjects his worshiper to a supreme test such as you would expect only at a very progressed phase of religious development. The more you consider the issue, the more puzzling it becomes. Is there a religious method in this madness?

In this narrative Abraham is only the executive or, you might say, the executioner of the Lord. Let us tentatively assume that the figure of the patriarch as well as his role is removed from the scene. What remains then of the story? That means, what remains of it when you put God in the place of Abraham? There emerges the tale of a God who attacks Isaac to slay him, the same violent and unpredictable deity that attacked Jacob when he crossed a river, the same God who attacked Moses in the night shortly after a son was born to him. (It seems strange that all those assaults appear as *rites de passage*.) Here is a primitive demon, not unlike the gods of Australian or African aborigines, who threaten to kill seemingly without reason.

Is it possible that the explanation connecting the scene

on Mount Moriah with the sacrifice practice of the Hebrews and their neighbors is only a superstructure? Or to
put it another way, that the sacrifice side of the story is
only a late interlineation or interpolation concealing another, ancient tradition? Is there a smoke screen around
the burnt offering of Isaac?

We now turn to the area of post-Biblical and rabbinical
legends embroidering the Genesis story. Those colorful
additions can perhaps provide us with some insights which
were denied to us in the study of the Genesis narrative.
Women state that the accessories worn with clothes often
say more about their wearer than does the dress. Our reassessment of the post-Biblical legends leads to some surprising impressions, which coalesce and attain the character of circumstantial evidence.

At the start of our review we said that in the legends
the original tempter is not the Lord, but Satan, the anti-
God. He is, we would guess, the representative figure of
an old, dispossessed and disavowed deity, the god of a past
pagan time, degraded now to a servant at the court of the
Elohim. This would tally well with the notion that the
original attacker of Isaac is a violent demon, the god of
savage tribes of the desert, not the Lord who says that the
heaven is His throne and the earth His footstool.

The God who orders Abraham to sacrifice his son is not
identical with the one who promises Abraham that he

will be the father of nations. He is not the "shield of Abraham" (Gen. IV:1), but one of his barbaric predecessors. He resembles more the gods whom the ancestors of the immigrants into Canaan worshipped. "Your fathers dwelt on the other side of the flood in old time . . . and they served other gods" (Josh. XXIV:2). Strangely enough, that demonic Satan speaks with the voice of kindness and sweet reasonableness and advises against the sacrifice of Isaac. We feel quite willing to give this devil his due.

We remember that Sarah, who does not play any role in the Genesis chapter, is introduced into the legends. Abraham keeps the intended sacrifice of their son secret from the mother, yet she cries and weeps at the separation and foresees that she will never see her son alive again. Abraham abducts or kidnaps Isaac and in some versions of the legends deceives Sarah. He tells her that the lad had to go away to be instructed by the priest Shem.

Here is certainly an anachronism, since we would not suppose that a boy belonging to a tribe of ancient nomads would be sent away to school. The feature that Isaac is supposedly taken to a teacher to learn the Torah, the law, belongs no doubt to a late period, perhaps to the time of the seventh century in which the Genesis tales were collected and brought into final form.

We suspect that behind this recent version another, much older, tradition is concealed—a tradition somehow

: 95 :

connecting the alleged sacrifice with some primitive tribal education of boys. Isaac could not have been a child any longer when he went on this three-day journey with his father. The Biblical story explicitly tells that he carried the wood for the burnt offering. We have to imagine him as an adolescent. The burnt offering is also brought into connection with circumcision in that legendary dialogue in which Ishmael boasts that he was circumcised at the age of thirteen years and Isaac replies that he would willingly let himself be sacrificed if the Lord commanded it.

This thought-connection suggests that the story has something to do with Isaac's circumcision. The operation was originally performed at the age of thirteen, while the Biblical story has moved it forward to the eighth day. Here is a contemporary adjustment to the custom of the period of the Genesis compilation. It certainly did not correspond to the practice of the patriarchal age. In the legends Isaac appears as a young man full of vigor. He is worried that he might push his father away when he wants to sacrifice him and thus frustrate the sacred action.

In some legends Isaac really dies and is resurrected. In others he emerges from the ashes after the burnt offering. We have seen that in a few sagas he returns with Abraham and the two young men—perhaps of the same age as Isaac —to Beersheba. In other versions, after the near fatal test, he is sent to his teacher, with whom he remains for three years to learn the Torah.

We were searching for the primal tradition underlying the Biblical sacrifice account; we hoped to discover appropriate material in the rabbinical folklore supplementing or replacing the Biblical account. What did we find there? Some features were, it is true, enlightening: Satan as originator of the temptation of the patriarch appears as the substitute for an older, degraded pagan god. The role he plays in the legends provides a fleeting glimpse of the kind of deity who demanded the sacrifice of Isaac.

The grief of Sarah at the separation from her son, her crying and mourning seemed at first only an addition to the Biblical leave-taking, but there is perhaps more to it. Other features are not in keeping with the sacrifice context at all, for instance Abraham's statement that Isaac, growing up, has to leave home to study. This trait belongs certainly to a time many centuries later than the age of the patriarchs.

The argument between Ishmael and Isaac seems to contradict the assumption that there is a link between circumcision and sacrifice of the son. In the legendary dialogue between Satan and Isaac, the Prince of Darkness argues with irrefutable logic that you cannot learn anything when you are dead, and Isaac will be dead. Isaac is rescued at the last moment. In some sagas he dies and is resurrected. How does all this fit into the context of the sacrifice tradition?

These and other thoughts emerging from the study of

the Genesis narrative and of later legends meet in a turbulent stream in our mind and threaten to clog the channels of thought. We are more confused and bewildered than we were before, and we numbly wonder how it all makes sense. The Lord who promised Abraham a numerous progeny demands the slaying of Isaac from whom alone Abraham's grandchildren can descend. The same God who insists on this sacrifice stays the hand of the sacrificer. Isaac dies, yet is resurrected.

Here are inexplicable and irreconcilable contradictions, flagrant inconsistencies and disruptive paradoxes. At first sight, the narrative seems logical and consistent; at second thought it is scarcely coherent. There is, as most commentators assert, a story of human sacrifice at its bottom; yet the sacrifice element has not an archaic but a recent character. It is contemporaneous with the age of the Bible-compilers and not with the age of the patriarchs.

The impression remains that this character is superimposed on a much older primal tradition which had perhaps nothing to do with the ritual of sacrifice, a tradition we cannot yet reach. When you listen to the Genesis narrative and to its modern commentators, it is as if you heard a loud voice proclaiming Abraham's loyalty and the mercifulness of the Lord who rejects human sacrifice. But when you then listen to the folklore of later sagas, you hear another whispering voice telling quite a different story.

All of a sudden the hopeless confusion into which we were thrown subsides and yields to clarity. A pattern forms itself before our eyes and rises out of the formless chaos. Some rifts tear the smoke-screen around the burnt offering on Mount Moriah.

The possibility of an interpretation that emerges is so dangerously daring and audacious that we hesitate to think it through to the end. Yet, as far as I can see, it contains the only possible solution of the problem. If it can be verified, it would mean not only the discovery of the primal tradition for which we searched, but also the possibility of flashing a light into the remote past of the people who produced the Bible two thousand years later.

CHAPTER IX

Death and Resurrection
in the Puberty Rites

—————— ❧ ——————

THE CHAPTER THAT FOLLOWS might seem to be a digression, but is in reality an attempt to pave a track through virgin territory to our destination. If we can control our impatience during the apparent detour, we will soon reach the end of this journey. A Viennese writer, Karl Kraus, once said: "It would not be so hard to get to Africa, but until you drive to the West-station that's another question."

Puberty and initiation rites mark the most important events in primitive and ancient societies and are of much higher social significance than marriage, childbirth and death. Among initiation rites the male puberty ceremonies are the most meaningful, since they mark the transition from boyhood to manhood, from a child to an adult member of the tribe. They are, to use an expression of van Gennep the *rites de passage* par excellence.[1]

The essence of those puberty rites is best characterized by the terms "death" and "resurrection." Those expressions are not used metaphorically, but have to be understood literally as applied to the thoughts of primitive man. This means that a boy undergoes several sometimes very cruel tests, is supposed to die as an adolescent and after some time to be reborn or resurrected as an adult man. The puberty rites are, of course, different in various societies and on different phases of social organization, but there are certain fundamental features that are astonishingly alike or similar in various civilizations.

There is the pervasive feature that the boys, at a certain age, are taken away from their mothers and sisters and are brought to a secluded place or sacred ground. In Australia, for instance, they are brought to a hut in the bush where they are taught the rules of the tribal code which they will have to obey and where they are introduced to the lore and traditions of their tribe. They remain in this elementary kind of private school for several months, in some cases even for a few years. During this time they are instructed by the old men of the tribe, often by its priests. They then return to their homes, but behave as if they were supposedly just born or reborn and have to learn how to walk and talk. They thus behave not as young men of thirteen, but as though they were "born yesterday."

Let me point out some significant features of this rite, to be found in different forms in all primitive societies. One common feature is the behavior of the mothers of the young candidates. All anthropologists and missionaries report that the separation of the sons from their mothers is very dramatic and often takes the form of kidnaping. D. F. Thompson, for instance, reports that a native of Cape York told him that the boys "are stolen from the mother."[2]

James G. Frazer[3] describes the way the Papuan adolescents are taken away to the forest where the initiatory rites are performed. The Australian women are told that a monster called Ballum will swallow up their sons and brothers. The mothers and sisters are thrown into deep mourning. "How then can the poor women be sure that they will ever see their dear ones again?"[4] They don't because the boys returning don't recognize them and behave as if they were strangers. When boys are admitted to the Kakian Association in the west of Ceram, they are led to the depth of the forest where a primitive shed is built. The high priest calls aloud upon the devil. Each boy who enters the shed after the priest is allegedly killed by the devil. As a testimony of his death a dull chopping sound is heard inside, a terrible cry rings out and a sword or spear, dripping with blood, appears on the roof of the shed: the boy's head has been cut off and the devil has carried him away. The mothers weep and wail since they are convinced that the devil has murdered their children.[4]

The Bukana mothers in New Guinea do not sleep during the night before the day of departure of the lads: "They cry continuously and caress and fondle their sons whom a terrible monster will devour in the morning."[5]

Similarly Isaac is taken away from his mother's tent when he reaches puberty and is brought to a secluded spot three days' journey away. It does not matter that the place in the Biblical report is a mountain called Moriah. We know that this name-giving is a late addition for the sake of glorification. Definiteness in myths does not prove historicity. It is most unlikely that nomadic clans living at the desert fringes took their sons there. (Perhaps tradition made Mount Moriah from a molehill.)

Like the mothers in the Australian tribes who mourn at the separation from their sons, Sarah is described in the legends as weeping and caressing Isaac before he departs.

She, too, doubts if she will ever see him alive again. In keeping with the higher state of civilization, the patriarch in the legends behaves more considerately than the Australian fathers: he either takes the son away surreptitiously without revealing the purpose of the journey, or he uses some pretext, such as the necessity of the boy's education.

The Australian mothers cry at the departure of their sons as if the boys were to die. That is not because the women equate departure with death (*Partir c'est mourir un peu,* say the French), but because they had been told that the sons were to be eaten up or killed by a malicious god or demon. Among some Australians the mothers mourn over their departed sons as one mourns over dead people. The belief in the death of the novices will be confirmed by the words of the tribesmen.

Among the Wiradjui tribes of Australia a group of men arrives sounding bull-roarers, beating the ground and throwing burning sticks.[6] In the meantime another group of men seizes the boys and leads them away. When the women are allowed to look around they see nothing but ashes and burning sticks. They are told that the monster Daramalun burned them when he came to take the boys away. Karl Weule describes the ritual of initiatory death among the Makua in Africa: the novices spend several months away from their mothers and from the villages.

By his long absence the son is considered dead in his mother's eyes.[7]

The Pangwe in Africa, whose puberty rites are described by Günther Tessman, mark their novices four days before the ceremonies with the sign called "consecration of God." The candidates are then taken to a house full of ants' nests and are badly bitten by the insects. Their guardian then cries, "Now you will be killed, now you must die!" The terrified boys are led to their "death" into a cabin deep in the jungle, where they live completely naked and in absolute solitude. After this they are painted white because they are supposedly ghosts. They return to the village, but they have to sleep in the cabin in the jungle for three months. Women are not allowed to see them eat because "the dead don't eat."[8]

Like these boys, initiates in other countries are also terrorized and terrified by the elders of the tribe who put the fear of god or rather of gods into them. They are threatened by mysterious voices and noises, and certain death is put before their eyes in the form of fire and weapons. Schellong emphasizes that the men of the tribe have "the unmistakable intention of thoroughly intimidating the trembling youth."[9]

There is no analogy to this terror in the Isaac story of the Bible, but we encounter it in the duplicate tale of Abraham's "horror of great darkness" that fell upon him at the occasion of God's covenant with the patriarch (Gen. XV:12). We find also another characteristic feature of the puberty rites, not in the Isaac story but in connection with the covenant. In most initiation rites the candidate obtains a new name, since he has been reborn. He has become, so to speak, another person. Thus the name of the patriarch is changed from Abram to Abraham. His grandson Jacob is called Israel after he is attacked by God at Peniel—a scene which is perhaps part of an initiation rite.

The potential death of Isaac at the sacrifice appears, as we know, as real death in some post-Biblical legends. It is said there that Isaac's soul vanished when Abraham took the knife or when Isaac lost a few drops of blood before the angel called. The Lord revivified him. In some sagas, Isaac's burnt offering is really performed and God resurrects the youth from his ashes. We find here the motif of death and resurrection, and we do not doubt that these rabbinical sagas contain vestigial remnants of the central concept of initiatory death followed by rebirth, a notion to be found in almost all initiation rites of preliterate people.

In pursuing the analogous features of the Isaac story and of the initiation rites, we found in both the separation of the adolescent boy from his mother, her grief and despair because she believes she will not see him again, his removal to a lonely sacred place, his alleged death and resurrection. We can recognize, in Yahweh's demand that

Isaac should be sacrificed, the Hebrew counterpart of the threat of the Balum monster to kill the Australian adolescent boy at puberty. It is, furthermore, easy to imagine that the sacrifice of Isaac replaced in the tradition the original rite of circumcision, performed at the puberty age. Both are bloody operations done with a stone knife. If the Biblical story is a distorted substitute for the description of a puberty ritual, then the placing of the story in Genesis is accounted for. It comes in where originally the circumcision rite of primitive people stood. The two ideas are akin.

In his article on circumcision Louis H. Gray expresses the opinion that in spite of the variety of motives all kinds of circumcision and subincision are ultimately reducible to the cause of sacrifice, "since initiation with its accompanying austerities may conceivably be regarded as itself a sacrifice to the tutelary deity."[10] G. A. Barton assumes that circumcision is a sacrifice to the deity of fertility.[11] To M. J. Lagrange circumcision is a rite in which a part is sacrificed.[12] Mircea Eliade contends that "since circumcision is equivalent to a mystical death the novice is believed to be killed by this superhuman Being."[13]

The closeness of the notions "death" and "circumcision" becomes transparent in African initiation ceremonies. H. Straube describes the operators who are dressed in lion and leopard skins to represent incarnate gods in animal form, the gods who in mythical times "performed initiatory murder." These operators wear the claws of beasts and attack the genital organs of the novices. The operators are sometimes called lions, and circumcision is expressed by the verb "to kill." Soon afterward the novices are themselves dressed in leopard or lion skins and they are restored to life. The sequence or rites thus suggests: circumcision —mythical death—resurrection—initiation.[14]

To quote an example of an initiation rite from our own continent: the rituals of the Mandan Indians culminate in the terrible hook-swinging of the candidates whose skin is first incised by a masked officiant. Their ordeal described by Mac Leod is the following: each boy has ropes attached to skewers that are applied to his body. With these he is raised on one of the four poles, suspended in the air in the Mandan lodge. He is naked. An attendant twirls the suspended boy around on his own axis. When he finally faints in the course of the twirling, the onlookers cry "dead." He is lowered and left lying on the ground outside the sacred lodge. When he dies (which very rarely happens) the Great Spirit is supposed to have taken him. When he revives, the Great Spirit has allegedly returned him to life. For good measure, the resurrected candidate has to make an additional offering to the Great Spirit by sacrificing the little finger on his left hand, a kind of displaced or symbolic castration.[15]

Even the substitution of animals for the novice to be killed is to be found in clear forms in the initiation rites of primitive tribes. To show that this is a crude and aboriginal representation, I have chosen an example from the puberty rituals of the Australians. The initiation ceremonies of the Yabim tribe of Papua (following J. G. Frazer's description) take place at intervals of several years when there are a sufficient number of youths to be initiated and when enough roasted pigs can be procured for the feast.

The principal initiatory rite consists of circumcision. The operation is performed in the deep forest in a long hut representing the belly of the monster Balum who is to swallow the novices. The old men of the tribe lead the procession of terrified boys to this monster. They raise a shrill song and sacrifice pigs to the idol "in order to induce him" to spare the lives of the candidates after they have been circumcised. The lads live for three or four months in the belly of the monster represented by the secluded hut. Sometimes, but rarely, one of the boys dies under the operation. In this case the men explain his disappearance to the women, saying that the totemistic monster has a pig's stomach and a human stomach and that unfortunately the deceased young man slipped by mistake into the wrong stomach and so perished miserably. In general the monster kindly consents to turn the candidates free and be satisfied with the roasted pigs the men offered to him.[16]

Quite similar are the rites of the Bukana and Tami tribes. The women and the uninitiated are told that the novices are swallowed by the Balum who, "however, is induced by the sacrifice of many pigs to vomit them up again. In spewing them out of his maw, he bites or scratches them and the wound so inflicted is circumcision."[16]

Among the Kai tribes a long hut in the forest represents the monster Alo. In front of the entrance to that hut a scaffold is erected. A man mounts it and makes a gesture of swallowing as soon as a novice is led to the scaffold. The trembling youth is now supposed to be in the maw of the monster, "but a pig is offered for his redemption and the man on the scaffold, the representative of the beast, accepts the offering; a gurgling sound is heard and the water which the man had just gulped descends in a jet on the novice who now goes free."[16] We would add many similar examples, but the few quoted here will suffice to show that since the substitution of an animal for a human victim as sacrifice to the god was known to the savage tribes of the Australian continent, such a substitution is characteristic of very ancient times.

It makes no considerable difference to our comparison with the Isaac story that in the Biblical case an adolescent boy is supposed to be slain as a burnt offering, while in the other case he is allegedly swallowed by a totemistic

: III :

beast. It is also not very relevant to our purposes that the animal substituted is a pig in the case of the Australian aborigines while it is a ram among the ancient Hebrews.

While there is no doubt of the intimate thought connection between sacrifice or sacrificial death and circumcision, another signpost points to a further discovery. We observe that the novices to be initiated in a group among the primitive tribes are mirrored in the Genesis story by two young men who are companions of Isaac on his journey. The primitive instruction or the education without books which the novices of Australian tribes receive in their period of seclusion has its counterpart in the Pentateuch saga. We recall that the boy's education is given as the reason for Isaac's departure in Abraham's dialogue with Sarah in the rabbinical legends; and that in some versions it is reported that the adolescent boy did not return with Abraham, but was sent to the priest Shem to be taught the Torah—the Do's and Dont's of the ancient Hebrew tribal code.

CHAPTER X

Reconstruction

THE VARIOUS IMPRESSIONS which we get from a comparison of quite a few hitherto neglected features of the Biblical Isaac myth and its later sagas with the essential parts of the primitive initiation rites, give rise to some tentative assumptions. They suggest that there are resemblances, until now undiscovered, between certain features of the Isaac tradition and the characteristics of puberty initiation. It is as if under the surface of the Genesis tale of Isaac's sacrifice other terrifying scenes became palpable. More than this: as if the account of that prevented sacrifice were a disguised and elaborate description of a primitive puberty ritual. Those impressions could be correct or could be founded on only apparent resemblances. They are, it seems to me, worthy of being examined.

Other impressions emerge from a critical revision of the modern exegesis of the Genesis narrative. I have arrived at the view that it cannot be an archaic account of a primitive custom of human sacrifice and of its abolishment, but rather that it is a relatively late story. It was perhaps composed at the time of the prophets who passionately attacked the contemporaneous practice of child sacrifice and its projection into the age of the patriarchs, and had the purpose of demonstrating that even in remote times the Lord considered human sacrifice an abomination.

My hope that the exploration of the Biblical and post-Biblical sagas will endow us with penetrating insights into the social and religious life of the prehistoric Hebrew clans has not been fulfilled. Our situation is similar to that of a traveler who, looking down from an airplane, has gotten an impression of the general character of the landscape below, and then sees individual houses, distinct areas and roads, when the plane descends and approaches the ground. The impression of a uniform landscape has vanished and we now discern differences where before we saw a whole picture, a general view.

As long as we looked at the scenery from the bird's-eye

view—as long as, to use the Old Testament expression, we moved "on eagle's wings"—the comparison we pointed out seemed very convincing. We easily crossed the abyss between continents and over the millennia. It was not difficult to compare the Hebrew clans of the second millennium with Australian primitive tribes of our time. *"Zeit und Raum nur ein Traum."* ("Time and space are but an illusion.")

But now we return to firm ground, to the familiar earth. We look around to find out where we are and to orient ourselves. In this moment all kinds of doubts awake and arguments emerge. Can we justify our venturesome hypothesis?

Let us remember how we stumbled upon those real or imagined analogies between certain features of the Biblical account and of the initiation rites. When we studied the Genesis narrative and the later traditions and legends something tugged at our mind, or rather at our memory. Another myth or mythological ritual much more primitive than the legends about the cattle-breeding patriarchs seemed to slip into the Rembrandtesque picture of the sacrifice scene. Are we justified in regressing to the rites of savage Australian natives living in the Stone Age while we investigate the custom of nomadic shepherds of the middle Bronze period of the ancient Near East?

In vindication of our venture, we can state that vestiges

of a much earlier and primitive Semitic organization and religion lived on in the oral tradition that led to the production of the Biblical stories many centuries later. Remnants and dim memories of old disavowed practices of a primitive past continued to live subterraneously all during the time the Hebrew clans migrated from the fringes of the desert into Mesopotamia and Canaan. They are perhaps still present, though not tangible, in the Isaac tradition. The oral tradition certainly changed them, and the Biblical stories, originating from that tradition, have come down to us through many different hands. Each of the later sources invariably transformed the tale as it was transmitted. Theophile James Meek in discussing those Biblical narratives pointed out that old mythical stories did not die and vanish; "they were retold, readapted, sometimes relocalized and mingled with others."[1]

The Bible is, we are told, a reinterpretation of early Hebrew traditions to meet the problems of a new age. It has its roots in those early group experiences of Hebrew fugitives drifting from the desert fringes into Mesopotamia and Canaan. To understand that development the scholars studied the conditions, the customs and religions of the ancient Near East countries.

In our search we traveled afield to study certain customs of societies that are in a cultural stage parallel to that of the Hebrews at the time of Abraham. Instead of remaining in the Canaan of the 18th or 17th century before Christ we were transported to the Australia and Africa of our time. Rather than occupy ourselves exclusively with the situation of the half-nomadic Hebrew tribes of that period, we explored the rites of the Papuans and other primitive people.

Such a deviation from the traditional methods of investigation, such an unconventional attempt at research, can be justified only if preceding work of this kind proves that its results are rewarding, and if the attempt made in this special case promises to solve problems which could not be solved by more customary methods.

An approach like this is certainly not as new or original as it first seems to be. Other research workers have used it when they explored the myths and stories of the Old Testament. James G. Frazer, whose books employ a similar method, advocates its principles in the following way: "Modern researches into the early history of man, conducted on different lines, have converged with almost irresistible force on the conclusion, that all civilized races have at some period or other emerged from a stage of savagery resembling more or less closely the state in which many backward races have continued to the present time and that, long after the majority of men in a community have ceased to think and act like savages, not a few traces of the old ruder modes of life and thought survive in the habits and institutions of the people." The eminent scholar states that there is no reason to suppose that the ancient Hebrews were an exception to this general rule, and he refers to the Old Testament in which such rudimentary survivals from a savage and barbarous past are preserved like fossils. "The comparative method, if I may say so, applied to ancient Israel, allows us to pierce the dead wall which, till lately, appeared to block the path of the inquirer."[2]

When we return to our particular problem of the Genesis tale, we are confronted with a jigsaw puzzle made of many fragments. Some pieces are missing, some are in the wrong place, and others, we discover, obviously belong to another puzzle. It has been our task to find the missing pieces, to correct the mistakes made in inserting some pieces into the wrong place and to remove those others that don't belong. This last work has been especially laborious since several fragments seemed at first to fit well into the picture, and we as well as other inquirers were long deceived until we discovered that they were misplaced.

One of the main arguments that can be brought against our comparison of the sacrifice tale with primitive initiation rites is the following: The burnt offering represents the religious act of a single person, while the puberty rituals of primitive tribes are festivals of whole groups of young men, mostly of the same age, who are led by old tribesmen to the secluded spot where the ceremonials take place.

To solve this contradiction, the development of initiation rites has first to be considered. In a brilliant book on the subject, Mircea Eliade, one of the world's authorities on comparative religion, has demonstrated that man of archaic society is what he is because of certain events that happened at the dawn of time and which are narrated in tribal myths. In the myths heroes or half-godlike persons appear, to whom all important behavior patterns and institutions are traced back. [The Polynesians assert, for example, that the different modes of deep-sea fishing were revealed to a mythical hero in primordial times.] Certain things, for instance circumcision and the ritual of death and resurrection, were events that first took place long before recorded history and were then re-enacted by each generation.

The novices in the initiation rites only re-enact experiences that happened to the cult hero, "in the dream time," as the Australian natives express it. "Since the initiation ceremonies were founded by the Divine Beings or the mythical Ancestors, the primordial Time is reintegrated whenever they are performed."[3] The novices thus become in some way contemporaries of the cult hero, whose adventures they repeat or rather re-enact in the rites. Here is a fundamental concept in archaic religion, namely that, as Mircea Eliade puts it, "the repetition of a ritual founded by Divine Beings implies the reactualization of the Original Time when the rite was first performed."[3]

The Genesis story of Isaac's near sacrifice represents in my view an excellent example of such a mythical tale, much changed and distorted in later phases of Hebrew tradition. On the surface the narrative accounts for the abolishment of human sacrifice and its substitution by an animal offering. Seen in the light of exploration "in depth," it reveals itself as the report of a primal initiation ritual in which the God of the "dream time" demanded the slaughter of a young man but acquiesced in the ram offered to Him, as a substitute or second best. Abraham— or his mythical equivalent—appears here as a typical cult hero or half-divine being who, as Genesis reports, not only performs circumcision for the first time, but to whom the ancient Hebrews owe the introduction of puberty rites.

That original tradition was superimposed later on with a secondary saga, in which Abraham became the first to replace human sacrifice with an animal offering. If my guess is correct this later legend, belonging to the age of Yahwism, was a transformation of a much earlier tradition whose features were altered in such a way as to fit into the newer tale.

Still other details were added later, for instance that Isaac carried the wood up the mountain for his own burnt offering. The localization of the scene on Mount Moriah is certainly an addition. Old details of the original tradition were omitted or reinterpreted and remodeled to accord with the secondary legend. Certain features, for instance that violence was done or intended to Isaac, tallied well with the essential and fundamental components of both stories since they are common to them. It is important to keep in mind the separation from Sarah and the departure to an isolated place.

If Abraham (or a figure similar to his) has within the saga the function of a cult hero, no further demonstration is necessary to show the connection between the sacrifice scene and an initiation rite. We have alluded to the remnant of an older tradition which also emerges, and in which a group of boys (represented in Genesis by Isaac and two young men) are led by an old tribesman or priest to the place of the initiation ritual.

The abyss between the most uncivilized aborigines of Australia and Africa and the half-nomadic Hebrews who had, at all events, reached some phase of culture, seems at first unbridgeable. Yet the tribal tradition whose reconstruction is here attempted does not originate in the age of the patriarchs (if we assume that they lived in the first third of the second millennium). It did not spring up in the time of Abraham who was the first Hebrew, that is, the first who severed himself from the conglomerate Semitic or Chamitic people who later included the Hebrews. That primal tradition reaches much further back, and has its deep roots in the ground of a common Semitic stock. It was only later on displaced by other traditions of patriarchal time, localized in Canaan and Egypt. That primal tradition originated in the pagan soil of the ancestors of the Hebrews who lived in Arabia or North Africa.

The oral tradition transformed into the Genesis story does not, of course, reflect the initiation rites as they were performed at the stage parallel to the primitive tribes of Australia or Africa, but in a very much changed form that was some thousand years remote from the prototype. Yet some last vestiges of the original rites are still vaguely recognizable in the late tradition. It is, to use a comparison, as if one discovered the family resemblance between a man and his great-grandson.

It is very possible that the secondary tradition in the shape of the sacrifice story was for some centuries well known among the Semitic tribes. It was, of course, not the story of Isaac, but that of an adolescent boy who was slaughtered on demand of the tribal god or demon. Such a myth belonged to the store of time-honored, established traditions.

What was the function of the compilers of the tales? One would at first think that theirs could not have been a very important task, considering that everybody knew the basic elements of the myth.

A young French playwright, Jean-Jacques Bernard, once told Bernard Shaw that the Parisians made "Saint Joan" a prolonged success in the theater.[4] The Irish author answered, "Oh, 'Saint Joan,' that's not a play by me. It existed; it had only to be written." Similarly, the legend of Abraham and of his intended sacrifice of Isaac existed for some centuries. When it was written—and very likely rewritten—the narrators made certain changes in it, adjusted it to the modified religious and social mores of their time.

There is, for instance, the statement that Ishmael was circumcised when he was thirteen years old, while the operation was performed on Isaac at the age of eight days. The practice of circumcision, which forms an essential part of primitive puberty rites, came perhaps originally from Africa and was spread, as Adolphe Lods suggests,[5] by the Egyptians among the Semites of Syria and Arabia, including some Hebrew tribes, at an early time. It is certainly older than the middle Bronze Age, supposedly the time of Abraham, since the Hebrews still used stone knives for the operation (Josh. V: 2-3; Exod. IV: 25). The Genesis narrative reports that Abraham introduced circumcision, and thus provides indirect evidence that tradition traces this custom as other ancient rites to the first Hebrew although it actually belonged to a much earlier phase.

It is very likely that the operation at the time when the Genesis story was finally composed was performed in infancy, but we know that it was originally performed at about the age of thirteen years [6] and was a preliminary to marriage. The report that Isaac was circumcised when he was eight days old (Gen. XXI: 4) is clearly anachronistic.

At the time of the patriarchs the transference of the operation to infancy had certainly not yet come about, and we are entitled to connect the circumcision rites with the sacrifice scene at which Isaac would have been thirteen years old; that is the same age at which Ishmael was circumcised. We must not forget that in the Genesis account the scene of Isaac's interrupted sacrifice is followed by the story of Abraham's search for a wife for his son.

CHAPTER XI

A New Lead

WE HAD BEST PAUSE here before descending to the last layer of investigation that we can reach. We set out to restore the original meaning of the Biblical narrative of Isaac's sacrifice. We paid close attention to the significant differences and to certain neglected features. We attributed a revealing value to that which Freud once called "the refuse of observation." In this way, so very much akin to the methods psychoanalysis applies in individual cases, we formulated the thesis that behind the Genesis story is the description of a primitive puberty ritual.

: 125 :

The most appropriate comparison to this kind of procedure would be that of discovering an original picture beneath some old canvas. This often results when a restorer tries to correct, for instance, the darkness of the varnish caused by the aging of the canvas. Such a condition of darkening often obscures the true colors of the art work. The restorer knows how to repair and preserve the picture. In the course of the restoration it sometimes happens that after the dirt and varnish are removed a concealed portrait emerges. In the work of restoration X rays, infrared photography, and ultra-violet light are used.

The application of these methods often yields evidence of abrasions and traces of repainting. X rays will, for instance, clearly show up spots repainted over the original, or they will reveal the existence of hidden holes and cracks that had been filled in and of places where the painting has been retouched. In former times the painting over of portraits was quite common. Perhaps the owner no longer cared for the subject of a picture in his possession and wanted something more interesting to himself.

Several interesting cases of this kind come to mind. The portrait of Sir William Butts hung for more than three hundred years in an obscure corner of the Butts family gallery in England. It was considered a mediocre painting of the Elizabethan period. A friend of the Butts' felt there was something peculiar about the hands of the person in the portrait, an elderly gentleman in the costume of the time of the Queen. The picture was subjected to X rays and revealed beneath the surface layer of paint the portrait of a much younger man. The original portrait had been painted by Hans Holbein, the Younger, in 1543. (It hangs now in the Boston Museum of Fine Arts.) A later artist had added about twenty years to the age of the model and had changed his costume to the court style of Elizabethan times.

On another occasion a painting representing John the Evangelist—a picture in the manner of Carlo Dolci (1616-1618)—was acquired by a Berlin collector. At the suggestion of Dr. Wilhelm von Bode, the director of the Berlin Museum, the overpainting was completely removed. The picture revealed beneath was a fine portrait of a woman by the Renaissance master Allessandri Alloi, known as Bronzino (1535-1607).

Another picture, now in a Berlin Gallery, was similarly restored. This painting had been ascribed to Andrea Meldolca, known as Schiavone, who was a pupil of Titian (about 1522). The middle figure in the picture was looking to the right and the men were wearing colored clothes. When the overpainting was removed, the middle figure was shown looking to the left and the men were dressed in black in Spanish style. The experts regard it now as the work of El Greco.

In a manner similar to that used by X ray specialists, we discovered beneath the story of Isaac's arrested sacrifice and redemption traces of a much older saga revealing the secret initiation rites of prehistoric Semitic tribes. Also we started from the task of restoring the original tradition of the Isaac tale and discovered that beneath the Biblical canvas another much more primitive portrait was concealed that had been painted over by a later artist.

What does the picture of the Genesis story show when the varnish and the overpainting are removed? We see a lad at about the age of puberty almost slaughtered by a god for whom the father serves as executioner. The sacrifice story reveals itself as a superstructure, as a Yahwistic addition and elaboration, as are various other features. Stripped to the first sketch, the original canvas presents the central scene of a puberty initiation.

At a very great distance from the scene we seem to see women. Can we not recognize in them the figures of the mourning, desperate mothers and sisters, who have to undergo a cruel and crucial test? When we visualize the scene—a young man bound on the altar ready to be sacrificed, his mourning mother collapsing from grief—another picture emerges.

I have boldly asserted that the narrative of Isaac's sacrifice takes the place of a primal tradition, handed down from one generation to the next. That is the puberty initiation of a cult hero; the oral tradition reported that once —in the "dream time"—a demonic god (whose place was

later taken by Yahweh) demanded that the young men
who reached a certain age had to be sacrificed to him.
Later on he was ready to acquiesce in accepting an animal
in their stead. In the original tradition it is certainly that
demon or God Himself who kills the boys. Only later did
he choose a deputy to take over the task.

The primal model of the whole procedure is, we remember, that monster, sometimes called Balum or Daramalun, who was supposed to kill and devour the novices
in the Australian puberty rites. Behind him appear the
old men or the tribal priests—representing father-figures
—who threaten, torture and finally circumcise the boys.

Having thus established the general concealed analogy
between the Genesis story and the primitive initiation
rites, we are still confronted with some unsolved problems.
We have to ask ourselves, for instance, what was the motivation for remodeling and reshaping the original tradition and for putting the other story in its place. But before all other questions we must ask what was the purpose
of that original tale.

To get an answer to those questions, we have to go back
to a phase much earlier than the one we assumed and to
some earlier source from which the tradition sprang. We
remember that, in the primitive puberty rites of Australian tribes, the vicious ghost or totemistic monster who
wants to kill the boys is also satisfied with the offering of

pigs in their place. This is the model of the substitution scene in Genesis. The primitive counterpart of the Biblical tale of that substitution is exemplified in the declaration of an Australian who was asked about the bloody appetite of Balum and about the significance of the tales about him: "We eat pigs and lie to the women."

Is there any doubt that there is an echo of that tune in the original tradition of the sacrifice scene? One of the purposes of that bloody tale was to frighten and intimidate the women and the uninitiated of the tribe. Is it possible that a similar heavy-handed prank gave birth to the solemn story of Abraham's sacrifice of Isaac? More than that, that it furnished the subject of hundreds of sermons in which the loyalty of the patriarch was praised by priests of three religions, and that Abraham's "decision" formed the cornerstone of Kierkegaard's existential philosophy?

Even the bull-roarer whose voice frightens the novices in the Australian bush has its Biblical counterpart in the instrument that is blown by the Israelites. This instrument, called the shofar, is made from the horn of the ram that had been slaughtered in place of Isaac.

Before our eyes now emerges in the place of the sacrifice scene on the mountain that other picture of a bloody initiation rite of Semitic clans of a prehistoric age. It is not the father who is tempted on this occasion. It is his adolescent son who is confronted with the hardest test of a primitive kind of education. That social and religious

ceremony also has at its surface a prank intended to fill
the mothers and the uninitiated with awe and terror.

We raised the question: Why was the sacrifice story put
in the place of a tradition of puberty rites in the Genesis
account? We can now give at least a tentative answer. The
compilers of the Pentateuch whom the Biblical scholars
call Elohist lived in the Northern Kingdom about 750 B.C.
This Elohist strand of the tradition begins with the introduction of Abraham as the traditional ancestor of the
Hebrews.

At the time when those writers prepared their account,
the fight against the practice of human sacrifice and the
attack against the custom of infanticide were at their
height. The lawgivers, the priests and the prophets stormed
together against that pagan practice which the Israelites
had taken over from the Canaanites and their neighbors.

The Biblical record written by the group of Elohist
compilers wanted to support the abolishment of child offering. In telling the story of Isaac's prevented death they
reminded their contemporaries that the Lord had already
repudiated that kind of sacrifice in the times of the patriarchal ancestors. It was a pseudo-historic argument thrown
into discussion in which the contemporary prophets declared that human sacrifice is an abomination before God.

The prehistoric initiation rites of the Semites were at
the time of the Elohists only a dim memory. The main
remnant or survival, still practiced, was circumcision, but

that had also lost much of its religious and social significance at the time of the eighth century. As the Isaac story shows, it had already been transferred from puberty to earliest childhood. Although still recognized as a token of the covenant between Yahweh and the Israelites, it was no longer understood as a puberty ritual and as the "preliminary" to marriage which it had once been.

We must not forget that the initiations were originally a carefully kept secret of the prehistoric Hebrew tribes. Only much later were they generalized to encompass the whole people. The newer concept of a covenant between the Lord and His people had already taken the place that the initiations had originally occupied. The primal tradition in which Yahweh had introduced the puberty rites had almost vanished. Traces of its faint memories were discovered by us in the elaborations and side-features of the Biblical Isaac story. This elaborated and re-interpreted myth had already dislodged the early tradition and was remodeled according to a contemporaneous concept. The primal tradition was submerged, but it had not disappeared.

The changes and distortions induced by Yahwism were certainly far-reaching and sternly incisive. Yet the repressed myth retained its emotional quality and re-emerged, many centuries later, in all its primordial freshness and spontaneity.

CHAPTER XII

The Covenant

WHEN LINCOLN WAS RE-ELECTED President in 1864 a clergyman in Middletown, Connecticut, displayed a sign in front of his house with the inscription: "And the Angel of the Lord called unto Abraham a second time."

The line is, of course, a quotation from the twenty-second chapter of Genesis. What had the Angel of the Lord to say to Abraham, who had just victoriously passed the hardest test of all men? The Angel said: "By myself have I sworn, saith the Lord, for because thou hast done this thing, and hast not withheld thy son, thine only son: that in blessing I will bless thee, and in multiplying I will multiply thy seed as the stars of the heaven, and as the sand which is upon the sea shore; and thy seed shall possess the gate of his enemies; and in thy seed shall all the nations of the earth be blessed; because thou hast obeyed my voice."

While the greater part of the Genesis chapter was composed by the editors we call Elohist, the verses quoted above immediately following the sacrifice scene belong to the older Yahwistic strand. They not only apply the name Yahweh for the deity; they also markedly differ in style and content from the other part of the narrative. Those verses, 16-18, seem to come forth from a frame of reference other than that of the rest of the chapter. After the pronunciation of that solemn promise of the Lord, Abraham then "returned unto his young men, and they rose up and went together to Beersheba."

An unprepared reader of the Bible might, at this point, ask in astonishment: Did not the Lord promise those great blessings before? He did, when He first called Abraham and ordered him to leave Haran, and again after the separation from Lot (Gen. XII: 2 and XIII: 15). When He made His covenant with Abraham (Gen. XV: 5) that promise was renewed. The covenant was re-established when the patriarch was ninety-nine years old. After Isaac's redemption, the promises were repeated in identical words, only this time with reference to how well Abraham had stood the test. That unprepared reader will ask: why the repetition here? Is it possible that the Lord did not remember that he had made the same pledge before?

The argument could be advanced that the faith and loyalty of Abraham gave cause to renew the promise. But this sounds more like a rationalization than a reason. Or were those previous promises invalidated when the Lord demanded the sacrifice of Isaac who was the only hope for progeny? This is, of course, unthinkable.

We hear, moreover, that the same promise and oath are renewed to Isaac himself in a situation similar to that of his father Abraham (Gen. XXVI: 3-4). We will discuss this and other duplications as well as the interchangeability of the patriarchal figures and stories later. Here we will restrict ourselves to some remarks about the odd fact that certain features we would expect to meet in the Isaac story are to be found in the Abraham tradition, and the other way around.

We have discovered certain essential indications of an old tradition of puberty initiations, concealed behind the story of Isaac's near sacrifice. To name a few: the notions of death and resurrection, the separation from the mother, the departure to an isolated place, the company of other young men, the education by a teacher.

Other points characteristic of primitive initiation rites
are not to be found in the Genesis saga of Isaac, nor in
the post-Biblical legends about him. They can, however,
be recognized in the Abraham tradition and especially in
situations analogous to those we constructed in the case
of Isaac. In other words, certain essential traits present
in initiation rituals are missing from the legends of Isaac,
but they are to be discovered in the life story of his father.
They are conspicuous especially in the Genesis account of
his covenant with Yahweh, which is the crowning experience in the life of the patriarch. In the Biblical tale
of the establishment of the covenant we find several elements which, in our interpretation, we would have expected to find in the scene of Isaac's sacrifice.

All the reports we have of initiation rites of preliterate
people agree about the emotional uproar among the novices
who are led to the place where they are supposed to be
killed by a cruel god or demon. The older men of the
tribe, representatives of the father generation, do their
best—or rather their worst—to intimidate and frighten
the boys. Images of cruel ghosts appear, mysterious voices
threaten the novices, who are subjected to all the horrors
of annihilation. Nothing of such a terrifying experience
emerges in the Genesis chapter telling of Isaac's walk
with his father to the place of the sacrifice. Only in some
post-Biblical legends is some panic in the boy mentioned.

: 136 :

In the Biblical account he shows scarcely any curiosity and just asks, "Where is the lamb for a burnt offering?" and seems to be satisfied with his father's information that the Lord will provide. "So they went both of them together."

During that near fatal journey of three days, all was quite peaceful and cordial. Even the commentators pay little attention to Isaac's feelings since they are concentrating on the emotional conflict into which Abraham is drawn. Only in Kierkegaard's interpretation is the fear of Isaac also considered. Nearly all Biblical scholars observe that the whole story is very reticent in mentioning the feelings of father and son; but it is conspicuous how willingly or obligingly the boy walks with his father up to the slaughter place—one might say like a lamb. The contrast with the terror and agony of the Australian and African novices during their march to the sacred ground, often described by anthropologists and missionaries, is very marked.

An intense emotion of such fright emerges in Abraham's experience before the covenant: "And when the sun was going down, a deep sleep fell upon Abraham; and, lo, a horror of great darkness fell upon him." (Gen. XV: 12). In the element of the deep sleep we detect a veiled expression of death that is often conceived in the initiation rites as magical sleep.[1] The horror in the patriarch reflects mortal dread when he is confronted with the approaching apparition of the Lord who, in this situation, as so often later on, manifests Himself in a symbolic shape. "And it came to pass, that, when the sun went down, and it was dark, behold a smoking furnace, and a burning lamp that passed between those pieces" (Gen. XV: 17).

The Lord emerges here in His old figure of the God of Fire, as He will later on in the theophany on Mount Sinai. In the solemn ritual of covenant-making the same two essential elements are found as in the experience of sacrifice on Mount Moriah: the slaughter of animals substituting for a human victim, and the fire, the burnt offering.

Another feature we would have expected to find in the Isaac story is not mentioned there, but is told in the context of the Lord's covenant with Abraham. That feature is the revelation of a new name for the patriarch. Giving a different name to the novice is one of the essential parts of primitive puberty rites. Since the boy died and a new male was born in the form of a baby, quite logically the new child has to be named. Among the tribes of Southeastern Australia, the new name is given to the novice immediately after initiation. That widespread custom symbolizing a new existence is found even among very primitive people such as the Hamana and the Halakwulup of Tierra del Fuego, whose puberty rites are extremely simple. W. Koppers, who attended those ceremonies of the South American Indian Yahmana in 1922, was given a new name to indicate that he was reborn into the tribe.[2]

When God renews His covenant with the first Hebrew and commands that every child should be circumcised, He says: "Neither shall thy name any more be called Abram, but thy name shall be Abraham: for a father of many nations have I made thee." (Gen. XVII: 5) Since the new name is connected with the introduction of circumcision for all members of the patriarch's household (Abraham and his son Ishmael are circumcised on the same occasion) the allusion to puberty rites is unmistakable.

Another feature of the puberty ritual is to be detected in the cycle of the Talmudic Abraham sagas, namely the instruction of the novice. Rabbi Jehuda ben Barsilai, commenting on the Biblical Abraham story, tells how God gave the young patriarch the Book of Creation, but Abraham could not understand it. A heavenly voice then spoke to him: "You can't grasp it by yourself. Search for a companion so that both of you can explore it." Thus, Abraham went to the teacher and priest, Shem, and stayed with him three years. We remember that the same years of apprenticeship are reported for Isaac in some post-Biblical sources. Here is the analogy to the long time spent by the adolescents in primitive societies in undergoing their elementary education.

We return to the question we raised at the beginning of

this chapter, namely the apparently arbitrary and contrived repetition of the covenant formula at the end of the Isaac narrative. With it we approach the troubling question of the very nature of the covenant, one of the pressing problems of the Old and the New Testament. In spite of the efforts of some generations of scholars who have grappled with this problem, we still don't know what is the origin and character of the covenant between the Lord and Israel. Only on the surface do things seem clear.

The expression "covenant" (from *con*: together and *venire*: to come) means a mutual agreement or consent of two or more persons to do or to bear some act or thing. In theology the word denotes the promise of God to man, usually carrying with it a condition to be fulfilled by man. It is generally assumed that covenants were originally made only among men and that the term was later transferred to the agreement between the Lord and His people. A covenant is, however, distinguished from ordinary agreements by several features. It is made under oath and is accompanied by solemn, often terrifying, rites. The oath is so essential for the character of the covenant that the expression oath is itself occasionally used as a synonym for it.

A covenant creates a new relationship between the parties, a relationship that did not previously exist. The covenant with the Lord, declare some scholars, is not an agreement of God with Israel, but one before Him. A covenant is usually binding to both parties, but it is also valid when it is imposed on one party by another or when it is assumed by only one party.

To digress for a moment from the world of the Bible to that of the nature-people of today, I would like to mention a kind of covenant (which is in fact called a covenant) existing among the Manu tribes in Africa. According to a recent work on the religion among primitives the Manus call the divine being they worship "Sir Ghost."[3] Their relationship with Sir Ghost is far from being a contractual one, but it is considered a covenant not to be thought of in secular terms. It is a solemn pact, moral in nature between men and the divine being. It differs very much from a merely secular contract, since there is no choice on either part in the relationship between the Manus and Sir Ghost. Their attention to him is of the nature of devotion. He on the other hand may not choose another ward than his own. The relationship is public and essentially of a moral character. At first blush it appears as if there is merely a trade for good fishing and health. On closer examination it is seen to be a solemn agreement and an important factor in maintaining public morality. The "force and sanction which make this agreement effective, are shame, guilt, scorn and sorrow."[3]

In Genesis the covenant of Yahweh with Israel—the Magna Charta of Judaism—is established and ratified and the penalty for non-observance is determined. The methods of covenanting as described in the Scriptures are various, but they are all in the nature of tests of obedience and endurance. The root of the Hebrew word for covenant is "Berith," whose Arabic root means "to cut." The expression originates in the primitive rites of sacrifice and blood brotherhood such as those reported in Genesis XV: 17 and Jeremiah XXXIV: 18f.

The nature and meaning of those rites have been penetratingly discussed by Robertson W. Smith,[4] James G. Frazer[5] and many other scholars.[6] Those experts compared the covenant rites with the bloody sacrifices of primitive people and ancient nations, and arrived at different theories about the significance of the ceremonies in covenanting. Yet in spite of many excellent insights the problem is still unsolved. Psychoanalysts, notably Géza Róheim and Arthur A. Brenner, and recently Dorothy Zeligs, have made meritorious contributions to the problem.[7] I do not pretend to solve the problem, but it can, it seems to me, be approached by methods combining comparative anthropology and Biblical scholarship and, last, but certainly not least, psychoanalysis.

The main difficulty, and one which is almost unsurmountable in the solution of the problem, is that we do not know the origin of the custom or of its ritual. The Biblical covenant is made either by a common meal, by a sacrifice of animals between whose divided bodies the partners to the covenant pass, or by some blood ritual such as sprinkling the blood on the partner. (God is often represented by the altar). Strictly speaking, there is no covenant between God and the individual, only a solemn pact or transaction between the Lord and the tribe. The patriarchs and later Moses are only representatives of the community, "united with one another and with God by participation in one life or lifeblood."[8]

It is the same blood that runs in the veins of the Lord and in the animals slaughtered at the covenant; in them is the sanctity of the same tribal life. Eating together of the same food or drinking the same blood, or even being sprinkled with the same blood, is in the view of the ancient Orient a sacred rite binding individuals together. "Only in this way can the sacred cement be procured which creates or keeps alive a living bond of union between the worshippers and their god."[8]

In this soil are the roots of many rites and practices widespread among ancient nations and primitive huntsmen. The rite of blood brotherhood is known all over the world. The simplest form of this sacred rite is that two men become brothers by opening their veins and sucking one another's blood. In William Robertson Smith's and in

James G. Frazer's books, as well as in the works of their successors, many instances of such blood-brotherhood rites and their variations are described. A purpose similar to that of blood brotherhood is, it seems, served in the initiatory rites. Some anthropologists think that the primary purpose of the Australian subincision is to obtain fresh blood which is a symbol of strength and fertility.[9]

Among the Dieri of South East Australia the men of the tribe open their veins and let the blood from them flow over the bodies of the novices to make them brave.[10] Among the Karadir and other Australian tribes, as well as the tribes of New Guinea, the novices have to drink blood.[11] As an explanation of the rite they say that the boys have to be strengthened with male blood because until then their blood had been that of their mothers. This is, of course, a secondary reason. The original meaning of the rite is a primitive kind of identification of the boys with the older men of the tribe, with the father generation.

In order even to begin to understand the original nature of the covenant, it is necessary to recognize the intimate connection of those blood rites with the rituals of covenant-making. One has at first to emancipate oneself from the modern concept of deity in order to conceive of those rites as uniting god and his worshipers. Spinoza said that if the triangle could speak, it would say that God is eminently triangular (*"deum eminenter triungularem esse"*). The deity of the Australian aborigines is a black fellow, if he is not a totem animal.

The tribal god is at the same time a universal one in the primitive stage of society. In this soil we have to search for the origin of the covenant idea. To use a comparison near at hand: for a little boy or a little girl there are no other parents than his or hers. The world of the baby is contained in its home. That is its orbit. That other children have parents is a comparatively late and only hesitatingly accepted notion. Originally there is no other "daddy," no other "mommy," than one's own. Nor is there another home.

The gods of primitive societies are not remote from the tribe; they are tribe members, in most cases also the ancestors of the tribesmen. They live among and near their own groups. Even in those cases where the god has withdrawn into heaven, he once walked the earth and belonged to his own clan. Also Yahweh took a walk in the Garden of Eden and spoke to Adam "as one man to another."

Radical changes must have evolved in the relationship between the tribe and its deity, since the god or the demon of the primitive society does not originally appear as a party or associate, as does his successor Yahweh in the covenant with Abraham. Can we guess the nature of those changes?

The Biblical scholars assure us that the Lord was originally conceived as a witness to the covenant-making and only later became a partner. I think that this interpretation cannot be correct. How could He have become the judge and the almighty avenger in case of non-obedience, when He had been their earlier only as a non-participating witness who had no share in the transaction? It is now almost generally assumed that the passing of both partners of the covenant between the divided bodies of killed animals had the significance of a conditional curse. Its meaning is, "If I do not keep the agreement, I will have to share the fate of those slaughtered animals." Who pronounces or threatens that terrible oath? Certainly the party who imposes the covenant upon the other, in this case Yahweh on the patriarch. Yahweh, then, is neither a witness nor an equal partner. Like Sir Ghost of the Manu tribes, He imposes the covenant and He threatens severe punishment should it be broken.

We can look, it seems to me, for the origin of the covenant in primitive initiation rites. Whatever the additional factors in the establishment of the covenant may have been, internal evidence supports my theory that its origin has to be found in totemistic initiation rites. Since the Hebrew word "berith" means "to cut," the notion of the covenant is almost by definition akin to the ideas of circumcision and bloody sacrifice.

The rites in covenant-making are essentially the same
as those of the initiation. There a blood union is established between the older men of the tribe and the novices
who now join their ranks. Certain rules and taboos are
imposed upon the boys, and they are told that they will
be thrown into the fire or otherwise killed if they do not
keep the orders and commandments taught them during
their seclusion. The gods or demons of the tribes often
pronounce the fierce menace.

The second common feature is the part circumcision
played both in the puberty initiation and in the covenant.
In spite of all later elaborations, it is still obvious that this
operation, as one of the most important events of the
initiation ritual, has been transferred to the eternal covenant. The children who enter the covenant of Abraham
have to be circumcised. Circumcision is explicitly called "a
token of the covenant betwixt me and you" (Gen. XVII:
11). Most important is Yahweh's demand that the uncir-
cumcised male child "shall be cut off from his people, he
has broken my covenant." That this operation is considered the essential part of the sacred pact, is proved by
the fact that the Jews still call the ritual of circumcision
"berith," which means "covenant," as well as "to cut."

The changes which I would guess have transformed
the puberty rituals into the covenant are of several kinds.
God became remote and retired into His heaven, although

He remained the deity of His people and they His wards. This relationship was obviously irrevocable. The covenant as a puberty ritual still demanded circumcision and the binding vow of obedience, but the initiation lost much of its significance when circumcision was put forward from puberty to infancy.

The most important change in the relationship between the deity and the worshipers was that Yahweh mellowed with old age and under the influence of cultural transformations. Thus also did His worshipers, for His transformation was determined by theirs. He lost His cruel, vengeful and barbaric character and became more and more a benevolent and protective father-figure, promising the Hebrews fruitful land and progeny if they were faithful to their covenant with Him. He still reserved vengeance as His privilege, but in the covenant His threats receded and His promises prevailed. The conditional oath or curse, expressed in symbolic form, still inveighed menacingly against non-observance of the sacred covenant, but the promises Yahweh held out to the Israelites outweighed the threats.

He also kept the old ritual although He had become invisible. The connection between Him and His people was still a blood ceremonial, as it was between the father and son generations in the puberty initiation. Although these rites were replaced by acts in which the whole people took part, the old forms remained essentially the same. The

Kuntamara ceremony in Central Australia, described by Spencer and Gillen,[12] can well be compared with the rites of the Biblical covenant-making. All tribesmen gather in the creek where the circumcised boys camp, and each man cuts himself with a sharp stone or glass. Each of the newly initiated boys does the same and then touches with a little of this blood the head of his father, and with a twig the head of a very old man called his grandfather.

Compare this ritual with the one described in the Exodus story (Exod. XXIV: 4ff). When the covenant between Yahweh and the Israelites is made, blood is sprinkled on the people and on the altar.

This is not the place to follow the development leading from the initiatory rites of preliterate people to the notion of the covenant. The most important part of this evaluation is not yet well understood. Another aspect of the covenant whose outlines I could detect in Hebrew prehistory is discussed in my book dealing with the blood union of God with the Hebrews at the place where it finds its supreme form: in the covenant on Mount Sinai.[13] The idea of covenant is connected with a solemn pledging of devotion to God. It is an unreserved, whole-souled commitment. On God's side it is a bestowal of grace upon men. The perpetuity of the covenant concerns also the seed of Abraham. As such, the covenant forms an enduring tie and a strong preserving force of Judaism.

It is a far cry from the solemn rite of the covenant—

from the rite of the sacred pact between God and his people—and the modern, almost businesslike relationship between the deity and the contemporary Jews. The incomparable actor Menasha Skulnik recently played the part of a tyrannical Jewish citizen of Syracuse in the comedy "The 49th Cousin." As the salesman, Isaac Lowe, a funny and pathetic character, he addresses God with easy familiarity and says in terms of a modern version of the covenant, "You stand by me and I'll stand by you!" When his colleagues at the temple reject him and two of his daughters rebel against him, he revokes the covenant and calls to the Lord, "At last, I'm finished with You, thank God!" The covenant is here treated as if it were an agreement in which one party can give notice to the other. It is in reality irrevocable. God cannot choose another ward and Israel cannot choose another god. In this matter Isaac Lowe overshoots the mark. A prospective son-in-law, a Gentile, tries to win over Mr. Lowe by announcing that he, too, has become an atheist just like the Jewish salesman. But Lowe does not let that pass and roars in anguish: "But you are a Christian atheist!"

CHAPTER XIII

Interchangeable Figures

THE APPARENTLY UNMOTIVATED repetition of the covenant formula after the arrested sacrifice of Isaac is not entirely accounted for by the idea that the covenant and puberty initiation are akin. We remember, too, that God had already promised Abraham an heir. He had said, "I will establish my covenant with him for an everlasting covenant, and with his seed after him" (Gen. XVII: 19).

Here, it seems to me, is the last gap we have to span before we can arrive at a new interpretation of the sacrifice saga in the Genesis chapter, namely the question of doubleness. The same promise is made to Abraham and to his son. The same story about introducing his wife as his sister is told about father and son in chapter twelve and chapter twenty of Genesis. There is the duplication of stories about the two patriarchs, and the wells they opened. Identical or very similar things happen to and are done by both the father and the son. A confusion of identities is barely avoided by some contrived or very artificial shifts.

There is a kind of looseness in the personalities of these patriarchs, an indefiniteness scarcely covered up, so that the two patriarchal figures sometimes seem to merge or to interchange their roles.

The Biblical scholars and exegetists have, of course, recognized this strange state of Biblical affairs and have tried to explain the resulting contradictions, repetitions and inconsistencies by tracing the twofold stories back to differences of the various compilers or narrators.

Some scholars have arrived, however, at a different explanation. I will quote only a few recent representative examples: John Bright contends that the historian dealing with the patriarchal prehistory is "moving in a realm of conjecture and theory."[1] Isaac was, in his view, the more primitive cult figure in the Negeb. The very remarkable (and in my opinion justified) conclusion this scholar draws is that Abraham has overlaid Isaac in the tradition. To support his theory Bright refers to the numerous parallels between Abraham and his son and to the paucity of material about Isaac. There are quite a few reasons why the tradition of Abraham overlaid and, in part, suppressed that of Isaac.

The two patriarchs were figures of essentially the same type, and their traditions were attached to the same locale. After Abraham's elevation to the position of Israel's first ancestor, all sorts of local traditions, for instance the story of Sodom and Gomorrha, were connected with him and cherished at his shrine.[2]

A similar view is maintained by John P. Peters who asserts that Abraham is particularly connected with the greater antiquity of Hebron, which seems to be reflected in the ancestral relationship of Abraham to Jacob. But why then, asks the rector of New York's St. Michael's church, "was Isaac connected with the still more southern Beersheba, the son instead of the father of Abraham?" His answer is that in the patriarchal stories Abraham and Jacob are much more vivid and real than "the more shadowy Isaac" and much more is told about them than about him. The importance of the sanctuaries of Hebron and Bethel accounts for the more active part which Abraham and Jacob play in Hebrew stories, compared with the "less vivid and less personal character" of the narrative of Isaac who is the hero of the more remote Beersheba.[3]

The genealogy in which Isaac is represented as Jacob's father reflects the peculiar historic relationship of Beersheba to Israel. It would have been impossible to assign the position of Jacob's father to Abraham, who was clearly so much older than Jacob. He must therefore become the father of Isaac in the complete genealogy. In Peters' view, the genealogy of the three patriarchs was determined by the three great primeval sanctuaries of the Hebrews.

Adolph Lods theorizes that each story of the patriarchal age originally had its own independent existence. "There was not always agreement as to which patriarch has been the hero of the story."[4] The fact that the same adventure is told twice, once in the life of Abraham and again in the life of Isaac, and that the digging of the well of Beersheba is sometimes attributed to Abraham, sometimes to Isaac, shows that there were variants of the same traditions. Lods contends that many of these adventures are ethnic facts, remembered experiences of clans, presented as the story of an individual. The tradition used "certain ancient names as pegs on which to hang stories originally unconnected with the lives of the persons in question."[5]

Martin Noth asserts that the patriarchal traditions were developed and transmitted in Palestine quite independently from the remainder of the Pentateuch.[6] It is probable that at one time each clan had its own patriarchal tradition of which we have only a small selection in the Bible. The figures of the patriarchs were revered as founders of the cult associated with certain places.[7] There is no evidence for our making any definite historical assertions or presuppositions about the time, place, and circumstances of the lives of the patriarchs as human beings. Not the individual figures, but the intimate relationship between the god and the clan was important. The promises of land and posterity may be assumed to have been an essential and original element in the type of cult whose founders the patriarchs were. Their original tradition was "not much concerned with their human personalities, but rather with the divine promises that had been made to them."[8]

It will be refreshing and invigorating to hear the voice of a great writer after our examination of the comments of so many Biblical scholars. In his beautiful lecture, given on the occasion of Freud's eightieth birthday, Thomas Mann expressed some decided views about the general problem of duplication in the Scriptures. The famous author points to the idea of the "lived life" of the Biblical figures. Their individual life appears as a succession, as a following in the footsteps of others. It is a kind of identification such as Joseph's teacher Eleazar practices in Mann's novel. For this figure "time is cancelled and all the Eleazars of the past gather to shape the Eleazar of the present, so that he speaks in he first person of that Eleazar who was Abram's servant though he was far from being the same man."[9]

The typical is for Thomas Mann the actual, the mythical.

The Ego of antiquity and its consciousness of itself was different from the modern one. It was less exclusive and less sharply defined. Ortega y Gasset says that man of antiquity, before doing anything, took a step backward: He searched for a pattern in the past into which he might slip and fit. Alexander followed the footsteps of Miltiades, and Caesar took Alexander as his model. This attitude is not identical with what we call imitation, it is rather a mythical identification, a kind of reanimation. Significant to life in antiquity was the reconstitution of the myth "in flesh and blood." Man found self-awareness, sanction and consecration in the myth.

Such consecration is found, for instance, in the life of Jesus who fulfilled that which was written. His words on the cross, at the ninth hour, "Eli, Eli, lama sabach thani?" express a lofty messianic sense of self. The phrase is not original, not a passionate outcry. It is a quotation from the Twenty-second Psalm in which the Messiah is announced and has the meaning: "Yes, I am He."

A feast is essentially an anniversary, a renewal of the past in the present. Every Christmas the divine baby is born again on earth to suffer, to die and to arise. In feasts time is abrogated. In the celebration a solemn narrative is acted out according to an immemorial pattern. Feasts of antiquity re-enact old occurrences and are essentially dramatic performances, scenic reproductions of stories of the gods with priests as actors, for instance of the life and suffering of Osiris in Egypt or of the Passion of Christ in the plays of the Middle Ages.

The profound remarks of Thomas Mann certainly reach the core of the problem of the duplication of Biblical stories, of the twofold elaboration of the same theme we so often find in the Scriptures. They bring us closer to the solution of the problem of the interchangeability of patriarchal figures, by pointing out that there is no sharp line drawn between the typical and the individual in myths.

The sacred rites are, so to speak, representations of what happened to the gods in primeval times. There is, furthermore, a necessary relationship of myths to rites. We can trace a myth such as that of Isaac's arrested sacrifice back to a certain ritual, in this particular case to the puberty rites of prehisoric Hebrew clans. When we restore the primal tradition of the myth, we also prove that the special features of the puberty rites determined its shape. The myth is finally revealed as the story of those rites in the oral tradition of the tribe.

There are at present two recognizable trends in the evaluation of the role of myth in religions. The one conceives of them as expressions of primitive *Weltanschauung* and attributes to them a central place within the development of religions. The other trend sees in myths a primitive manifestation of a groping intellect, and strives in the direction of a "demytholization" of religion. I do not share either of these extreme views and am here only interested in tracing the Isaac myth as far back as possible.

In his important book, *Lectures on the Religion of the Semites*, first published in 1889, William Robertson Smith offered a new concept of the place of myths in ancient religion. Mythology, which takes the place of dogma in all religions of antiquity, had no sacred sanction and no binding force on the worshipers. Myths were merely part of the apparatus of cults. The individual was offered a choice of different accounts of the same event and no one cared which one he accepted. It was not obligatory to believe in a certain myth. What was demanded was the exact performance of certain sacred acts we call rites. Smith contends that in almost every case the myth was derived from the ritual and not the ritual from the myth. The rites were fixed and the myths were various. "The ritual was obligatory and faith in the myth was at the discretion of the worshiper."[10]

Even more energetically than William Robertson Smith, J. G. Frazer formulated the opinion that "ritual may be the parent of the myth, but can never be its child." He asserts that "while many cases can be shown in which a myth has been invented to explain a rite, it would be hard to point to a single case in which a myth has given rise to a rite."[11]

Although this derivation is now almost generally accepted, we have very few recent examples of scientific analyses of a specific myth whose features are traced back to certain parts of an ancient ritual.[12] Our psychoanalytic exploration of the Isaac myth continues the research work of J. G. Frazer and William Robertson Smith.

The observance of certain rites was the essential core of ancient religions. It remains even today the most important manifestation of faith for the majority of people.[13] The belief in the stories of the Scriptures and in dogmas is of comparatively minor significance. Gretchen in Goethe's *Faust* catechizes her sweetheart and tries to find out what he thinks about religion. When he assures her that he reveres the Holy Sacraments she says:

> But without desire, alas,
> It's long since you confessed
> or went to Mass.

Religion has become more and more diluted and its zeal has been reduced to room temperature. Although religious belief has finally reached that anemic phase which George Gissing once characterized in a certain British type whose religion "strictly speaking is an irradicable belief in his own religiousness,"[14] the practice of ritual has not diminished.

CHAPTER XIV

Hebrew Origins and Initiation Rites

———— ❧ ————

I T IS POSSIBLE, though unlikely, that archaeology will
find some evidence for the historicity of Abraham,
but even if the existence of that first Hebrew should
prove a fact, the concept that he was a monotheist, abolished human sacrifice and replaced it by animal offering,
will remain the expression of an imaginative faculty that
puts the fantasy of fairy tales to shame. The idea of a

test of Abraham's faithfulness in confronting him with Yahweh's demand is, of course, utterly anachronistic and has to be attributed to compilers of the time of King David.

It is noteworthy that one rarely hears utterances of astonishment that that "grim story" was included in the Scriptures at all. Just as I am writing these lines, an article in the *New York Times*[1] reports that the Reverend Dr. David Seligson gave an interpretation of the Isaac story in his sermon in the Central Synagogue and confessed that he found it "unintelligible as a child, incredible as an adult," and as a father he must regard it as "impossible." He characterized the submission depicted in the Biblical story as "the unquestioning acceptance of what had been handed down and the readiness to countenance any kind of barbarism or inhumanity in its name." To Dr. Seligson, who advocates "Judaism by consent and not by submission," the religious commitment of free men and women expresses "the inquiring spirit prepared to question and to change, to challenge that which no longer commands our intelligent consent." The question of how that story found entrance into the Bible is certainly one that challenges the "inquiring spirit."

The Bible is, as it is well known, not a book, but a collection of books, or rather a collection of scrolls. The word Bible comes from the Greek through Latin and means "books" in the plural. However early one dates the first writing of the Biblical stories, one always presupposes a long preceding phase of oral tradition, at least a period of a thousand years.

The term "oral tradition" in its vagueness and indefiniteness is often cavalierly applied by Biblical scholars and commentators, who find in it a wide playground for fantasies. There are "more things in heaven and earth" than Biblical scholarship has dreamed of with regard to the nature of the Lord and His divine predecessors in Hebrew origins.

In undertaking the journey into the Never-Never land of oral tradition, one must start from that layer of the Old Testament which the experts recognize as the oldest. That means those parts of the Pentateuch that are, in their opinion, the earliest to be fixed in written form. These oldest pieces are, according to general agreement, not prose, but poetry—songs praising or celebrating contemporary events—for instance Deborah's song (Judg. V), to be dated not later than the eleventh century B.C.

The scholars are, as one of them declared,[2] struck "by the resemblance between the bards of the Odyssey, Phemius and Demodocus, singing to the lyre in the halls of chieftians, and the fragments of primitive songs preserved in the Bible." The difference is only in the scenarios: it is not the almost feudal banquet in the hall of the noble, but the tribal gathering of the people around the well (Num.

XXI: 16-18; Judg. V: 11). Other scholars imagine the tribesmen sitting in their tents or around campfires telling the stories which appeared later, elaborated, in the Bible. Here, according to Biblical historians, is the source of primal traditions.

I am ready to contradict all these theories about the origin and character of the oral tradition. I assert that only one place and one occasion are imaginable as the soil from which it springs and on which it was handed down from generation to generation: namely the tribal initiation, or rather the religious and national institutions that originated in these rites and finally replaced them. The initiation rite was the primal source of what was later on developed into an oral tradition, and it relates to a period in which the Hebrews, as an ethnic group, had not yet been separated from the Semitic stock but still lived among the other clans in Arabia or in North Africa. That means to a time not reached by archaeology. Yet faint traces of those immemorial rites remain indelible, so that we can discover them with the methods of archaeological psychoanalysis.

We invade here an area unknown and until now unknowable, but one whose existence has to be deduced from unescapable assumptions. The "oral tradition"—I am using this term provisionally—was a store of adventures of the gods or the tribal forefathers, of cosmology, folklore, tribal customs and laws as well as of accepted modes of behavior taught by the older men or the priests during the initiation period of adolescent boys. Here is an unorganized conglomeration of apparently disjointed disciplines; yet it is an effective method of primitive education. This is the place and the frame within which the tribal sagas as well as the tribal customs were transmitted in preliterate societies. Since religious and social codes are identical in this stage, and since the history is essentially that of the tribe, the novice "learns" almost everything he needs to know in order to live as a member of his primitive community.

The nucleus of those traditions which have come down to us in the form of the Pentateuch had been conveyed to the youth of the prehistoric Hebrews during their initiation period. The comparison of the source of the oral tradition with the songs of the Odyssey, and the analogy with the customs of the Bedouins of today, will not help us to penetrate the core of prehistory. We have to go further back and search for the origin of the Biblical sagas in the world of primitive and preliterate societies.

I am leaving aside a discussion of the tribal codes and their comparison with the "commandments" of primitive tribes because I have dealt with this subject in a previous book.[3] I will speak only of the patriarchal stories to which the Isaac episode belongs, comparing their origin with those sagas which are presented to the novices in their instruction time.

The history taught to the novices shows them what happened to their ancestors, often half-divine beings, in primeval time. The youths encounter those cult heroes and witness the mythical events. The following example of that part of the primitive puberty ritual reflects the character as well as the form of the so-called oral tradition that continues to live in the Genesis narratives.

The Kurnai tribesmen of Southeast Australia cover their novices with rags and make them fall asleep with the help of monotonous songs. During the sleep the candidates are equipped with the "belt of manhood." Soon thereafter begins their instruction, the central part of which is called "showing the Grandfather." The novices lying on the ground with their heads covered with rags, hear the whirling bull-roarers approach. The novices are told to throw off the rags and to look at the sky. Then the bull-roarers are shown to them. Two old men tell the boys: "You must never tell this! You must not tell your mother, nor your sister, nor any who is not jeracil (who is not initiated)!"

One of the bull-roarers is larger, the other smaller, and they are introduced to the novices as "man and woman." The boys then hear the myth of the origin of initiation. In the primordial time a Divine Being, Mungan Ngaa, lived on earth. He instructed the Kurnai; his son Tundum is considered the ancestor of their tribe. The two bull-roarers shown to the boys were named after him and his wife. Mungan Ngaa introduced the initiation mysteries and his son performed the circumcision for the first time.

After the revelation of this mystery the teaching is continued in the camp. The novices attend there a series of dramatic or pantomimic presentations of the great events in the mythical time. This instruction—simultaneously religious, moral, and social—goes on during the many months the novices remain with their tutors on the sacred ground. The myths and the names of the Supreme Being and the events in primeval times form the quintessence of this simplest, but perhaps oldest, Australian initiation.[4]

The various forms of the puberty rites show, in spite of all divergences between the different tribes, a stereotyped pattern. The "oral" part in them is certainly not the most important and is perhaps the result of a progressed phase. Eliade emphasizes that "the dramatic and choreographic recapitulation of the primordial events is a theme common to all Australian initiation."[5] To use a comparison, children "play" or act events before they tell stories of what happened. They imitate and re-enact also the behavior of adults in their play.

Myths are performed before they are told. They are enacted, accompanied by gestures and some words that provide the commentaries of the older tribesmen. The representation of tribal history is made to a great extent in dancing and gesticulation. The "oral tradition" of which scholars speak does not mark the beginning, but rather the second phase, of that mass communication.

All the world of primitive myth is a stage. The actors are often the priests and "one man in his time plays many parts." They act not the seven ages of the individual, but "this strange eventful history" of their tribe.

It is not easy to imagine that the tales of Genesis, and especially the patriarchal stories, were once performed, were of the nature of "mythic enaction," as the scholars say. To us who are accustomed to reading and hearing those sagas, this seems to be as odd as, let us say, a production of Hamlet in a silent movie. Yet in this tragedy is a play within the play, performed in pantomime and accompanied by the comments of the Danish prince. Thomas Dawn Heald made it plausible that the prehistoric Semites, to whose group the later Hebrews belonged, had given dramatic presentations of the Genesis stories quite similar to the performances of Australian rites. In both primitive forms the adventures of the ancestors or cult heroes were presented.

The primitive "formal" education in the Australian puberty rites makes the boys familiar with the history of the group, but at the same time forcefully subdues their rebelliousness. They learn to obey the rules and regulations of the tribe and are made aware that disobedience has the consequence of death. All communications during the time they are secluded in the bush—comparable to our camps for adolescents—are top secrets of the initiated and it is severely forbidden to divulge any part of them to the women and the uninitiated. That must also have been the case with the prehistoric initiation rites of the Semites.

The later development of this situation can only be guessed. There is almost no indication as to which form it took, but—to quote Sir Thomas Browne—"What song the sirens sang, or what name Achilles assumed when he hid himself among women," though puzzling questions, are not beyond conjecture.

My hunch, presented elsewhere, is that when the secrecy about the puberty rites was dropped, or rather when those rites were extended to the whole people, the name of God as well as His countenance became secret.

We have quoted one representative example from an Australian initiation in which the novices were told how a god once introduced the ceremonials. Similar myths from African, American and other Australian initiations could be added. They would add weight to the notion that in puberty rites the vicissitudes of the tribal ancestors were re-enacted, and the introduction of the rites was traced back to a god or a cult hero. Is it very difficult to imagine that the prehistoric Hebrews had similar traditions during

: 169 :

the phase of primitive clan society, and that one of those traditions is preserved in the altered form of the Biblical Isaac story?

We are, of course, aware that the ancient Semites who roamed the fringes of the desert had advanced a few thousand years beyond the phase in which the Australian and African natives live. When the ancestors of the nomadic Hebrews entered the stage of history, they were no "savages" in the anthropological sense. Even in the patriarchal phase, that is, around the first third of the second millennium, the old puberty rites had lost much of their scope. In the prehistoric period circumcision represented the initiation ritual and, as the Exodus narrative proves, even this rite was for some time not observed and had to be re-introduced.

Several reasons why puberty rites moved into the background can be guessed. There were the migrations of the Hebrew clans, their struggle for place and pasture, their oppression by the Egyptians, their fights with the Canaanites, and finally their increasing assimilation with the more advanced civilizations around them.

All these factors were unfavorable to the retention of primitive customs. As a result, the central place and significance the initiation once had in the prehistory of the Hebrew tribes were transferred to the notion of the covenant with Yahweh.

As we have seen, many of the essential features of the ancient puberty ritual had been absorbed in the idea of that covenant in which the kinship between Yahweh and the Israelites was confirmed and solemnly renewed. Circumcision as a "token of covenant" still played the most important role in the continuation of the initiation. The puberty rites had been extended to the whole people, who became a nation of priests in that sacred mass communication on Mount Sinai.

The patriarchal sages were in much more primitive form when they were first transmitted to the adolescents who became members of the Hebrew tribes in the initiation phase. Just as some fundamental parts of those traditions persist in vestigial traces in the Genesis account, so also did the oral traditions develop and appear later, much altered, in the Bible.

The patriarchal sagas are thus the written successors to the dramatically presented myths of Semitic prehistory. Their material was taken over by priests and scribes, storytellers and compilers, who continued the work of the tutors of adolescents in the seclusion phase of initiation. The Bible, as heir to the task of instructing the boys in preliterate Israelite society, became not only the pedagogue but also the history teacher of all Israel. It became, so to speak, the textbook of adult education par excellence.

The puberty rites became obsolete and were later revived in the transformed and diluted form of the Bar Mizvah celebration. All education and knowledge of tribal history, as well as the codes of the people, were now communicated with the help of those scrolls on which the remnants of racial memories were inscribed.

Even in a very late phase those sagas were not simply read but were recited or even sung, and the students memorized rather than "learned" them. Those scrolls were still spoken of as of the Torah, which means "law," as though they still continued the primitive lawgiving of the initiation.

We have followed the development of the Bible not only as far back as its beginning from "oral traditions," but much farther back to its embryonic stage two thousand years before those traditions were written down, before they became the "Scriptures." When we admire the superb prose of the Bible, we should not forget that in it is an audible echo of the dramatic performance of the sagas first enacted in the initiation festivals of a prehistoric past.

PART THREE

FROM ISAAC
TO JESUS

———— ❦ ————

YET IT PLEASED *the LORD to bruise him; he hath put him to grief: when thou shalt make his soul an offering for sin, he shall see his seed, he shall prolong his days, and the pleasure of the LORD shall prosper in his hand.*

He shall see of the travail of his soul, and shall be satisfied: by his knowledge shall my righteous servant justify many; for he shall bear their iniquities.

ISAIAH LIII: 10, 11

CHAPTER XV

Moriah and Golgotha

ⅠN A RECENT WORK Joshua Adler characterized Isaac as "the absolute sacrifice all during his life which had been at that moment on Moriah. He gave his entire life and activities over to adherence to the one and only Lord." In contrast to his father, who was active and aggressive, Isaac shows a "mystical detachment" from all life.[1] The sermons of Christian and Jewish priests do not frequently deal with the story of Isaac's sacrifice. Even more rarely is the personality of the patriarch discussed in them.

According to the *New York Times,* a senior rabbi recently said in a sermon that Isaac, although essentially undistinguished, nevertheless performed a highly meritorious act. "Though like the average unoriginal, uncreative, unworldly dreamer, Isaac fulfilled the sacred duty of preservation." Abraham had dug the land, the wells, but later the Philistines caused them to cease to flow. Then Isaac reopened these wells to restore the land's verdure. The rabbi declared that "the same sacred duty of preservation of their inheritance is for all men until comes the time for new advances." He concluded that we average people, "the garden variety, might do well to consider whether we could say at the judgment, as could Isaac, that at least we did not retreat, but held fast and did what we could to keep clear the springs of life."[2]

Even such examples of allegorical exegesis of Isaac's story are seldom heard from the pulpits of churches and synagogues.

The figure of Abraham's son, willing to give up his life on the altar, is clearly that of an obedient victim. The post-Biblical legends paint his character as meek, and emphasize his kindness and tenderness. In the Jewish Daily Morning Prayers (Selichoth) he is called "the tame dove."[3]

Erich Wellisch justifiably points to the absence of aggression In Isaac's character and calls him "the first of the great kind ones" of Biblical history, followed by Hosea and Rabbi Hillel and finally by Jesus of Nazareth Himself.[4]

The resemblance to Christ in the patriarch's nature and in the situations in which he appears in the Genesis story was early recognized. Even certain details common to both Biblical tales show striking similarities between Moriah and Golgotha and even Gethsemane. For example, the two young men whom Abraham took with him on the journey were left behind when the patriarch and his son began to ascend the sacred mountain. "Abraham said unto his young men, 'Abide ye here with the ass; and I and the lad will go yonder and worship.'" (Gen. XXII: 5). The analogous situation is found in St. Matthew's story in which Jesus says to his disciples, "Sit ye here, while I go and pray yonder." (XXVI: 36).

We just mentioned the ass in the Biblical tale of Abraham and Isaac and are thereby reminded that the animals in this saga had a special significance. The Genesis story reports that Abraham, after having received the divine commandment, "rose up early in the morning and saddled his ass." The rabbis pointed out that Abraham himself and not his servants did the saddling. The ass seemed to have been granted an extremely long life. According to the post-Biblical legends it was created at the dawn of the sixth day of creation which preceded the first

Sabbath of the world. It was then used by Moses who set his wife and sons on it when he returned to Egypt. It was the ass on which, according to the prophecy of Zechariah (IX: 9), the son of David would triumphantly ride into David's city.

Like the ass, the ram was created in the twilight of the sixth day of creation because God foresaw the role it would play on Mount Moriah. The animal was already grazing under the tree of Life. When the time came, an angel brought the ram from Paradise to the thicket on Mount Moriah. Rabbi Chanina ben Dosa pointed out that the remnants of the ram were destined to accomplish great things. From its ashes the inner altar of the Temple was built and the strings of David's harp were made from its sinews.

Yet a more significant role was reserved for the ram. The church fathers saw in it a symbol of the redeemer. St. Cyril of Alexandria courageously stated that "the ram represented the figure of the Cross."[5] St. Athanasius of Alexandria asserted that Abraham, "having been restrained from sacrificing Isaac saw the Messiah in the ram which was offered up instead as a sacrifice to God." Yet the Messiah seen in the ram "was the suffering and redeeming Messiah prophesied by Isaiah."[6]

The church fathers were eager to compare the Genesis narrative of Isaac's prevented sacrifice with the Golgotha report. St. Cyril of Alexandria, just before mentioned, remarked in his third Dialogue of Theodoret that in both situations a father and a son bear the material for the sacrifice, and that the place for it is similarly a mountain top. In both events the leading characters, Isaac and Jesus, die—to be resurrected after three days. St. Athanasius of Alexandria refers to a passage in the Epistle to the Hebrews (XI: 17-19) in which it is said, "By faith Abraham, when he was tried, offered up Isaac: and he that had received the promises offered up his only begotten son, of whom it was said, That in Isaac shall thy seed be called: Accounting that God was able to raise him up, even from the dead; from whence also he received him in a figure."

In his *De Civitate Dei* St. Augustine compared the thicket in which the ram was caught with the crown of thorns worn by Christ.[7] Isaac as well as Jesus carried the wood for the sacrifice up the mountain, Isaac the wood for the burnt offering, Jesus his wooden cross. Precopius of Gaza hears an echo of the words of the angel in a passage of the gospel of St. John. The angel said to Abraham: ". . . and hast not withheld thy son, thine only son." The Gospel of St. John says "For God so loved the world, that he gave his only begotten son." St. Paul (Rom. VIII: 32) says of God, "He that spared not his own Son, but delivered him up for us all."

Irenaeus described Abraham "having with a willing mind yielded up his only begotten and beloved son to God, in order that God might be well pleased on behalf of his seed, to grant his only begotten and beloved son as a sacrifice with a view to our redemption." Abraham thus seemed to have set a precedent, and his willingness to sacrifice Isaac created a model for the great deed of supreme self-denial.[7]

This also seems to be the view of St. Ambrose, who compared the near sacrifice of Isaac with the Passion of Christ and said, "Isaac is therefore the prototype of the suffering Christ." In his Epistle (II: 21) James, the brother of Jesus who became the first bishop of Jerusalem, said, "Was not Abraham our father justified by works, when he offered Isaac his son upon the altar?"[7] Abraham, says James, did not meditate about his duties toward God, but he carried out the commands of the Lord. In the Epistle of Barnabas it is said that the sacrifice of the Saviour accomplished the event of Isaac's prevented sacrifice.

In an excellent article, Israel Levi has described how the church especially in the second century untiringly compared Isaac's death with the sacrifice of Jesus.[8] The scholar refers also to the post-Biblical legends from which the church fathers took their material for the comparison, for instance the story of Isaac's resurrection. Here the

Halachoth, collections of traditions regulating the conduct of the Jews according to the Talmud, came into their right. We heard that according to some legends Isaac died and was brought into paradise in order to be cured from the injury inflicted by his father before the angel stopped him. A Midrash by an unkown author is quoted to the effect that Isaac was burned to ashes and then brought back to life.

The Zohar refers to Isaac's temporary sojourn in paradise. According to Caro's Toledot Yizachak even the ram came to life again after having been burned to ashes. This ram, says another source, had been the bellwether of Abraham's flock. The significant detail is added that Abraham called this pet animal Isaac, and it was therefore quite appropriate that it should take the place of Isaac the boy.

Only a few remarks about the scenario should be added. In the Genesis story Abraham calls the place of the intended sacrifice Jehovah-jiveh which means the Lord will see, will provide. The Talmud finds all kinds of meaning in this name-giving. According to Berakhot V, of the Babylonian Talmud, Sem had originally called this same place Salem, or Peace. God then combined the two names given by Sem and by Abraham, and called the place Jeru-Salem. Friedrich Delitzsch points out that the distance from Beersheba to Moriah which Abraham,

Isaac and the two young men walked is about thirty-eight miles which would correspond to the three days attributed to the journey in the Biblical story.[9]

In broad outlines these are the external threads connecting the legends of Mount Moriah and of Golgotha, as they were followed by the church fathers whose anti-Jewish attitude did not prevent them from using rabbinical saga material. There are certainly also internal strands running from the patriarchal tale to the story of the Passion, and some of them reach even further back into the prehistoric Semitic mythology.

Not all modern historians pursuing those threads are without bias, and not all of them come to conclusions that appear justified. Arnold Toynbee[10] for instance compares the three stories of King Mesha's sacrifice of his oldest son as burnt offering to Chemosch upon the wall (II Kings III: 27), Abraham's arrested sacrifice of Isaac to Yahweh, and God's acceptance of His son's sacrifice to Himself, the Father. In Toynbee's view the three performances are virtually the same act, yet the first and the third of them are spiritually at opposite poles. Mesha's son is an unwilling victim, Christ's deed is a sacred sacrifice of Himself, and Abraham's son yields to necessity. His sacrifice links those two morally antithetical extremes. This sounds plausible and the historian's presentation is, at least, on the surface, logical, but is it psychologically correct?

To Toynbee the three acts are virtually the same because he considers them only from the point of view of sacrifice, or he sees them as three forms of sacrificial death. When we look at them from another angle, however, they no longer appear as "virtually the same acts." Since all three cases have to do with violent death, let us tentatively replace the notion of sacrifice with the term of murder. Seen from this viewpoint, Mesha's deed is a father's murder of his son; Abraham's act is an intended and prevented murder, and Jesus' death is the result of self-murder or suicide. Only very superficially can the three cases be seen as "virtually the same."

In contrast to the two preceding parts of this book, this last part will not treat the subject fully. I will only present some especially interesting aspects of the comparison between Isaac and Jesus, only the highlights of the two sacred stories. I shall offer those features that are still obscure and arouse that "holy curiosity" of which Einstein often spoke.

CHAPTER XVI

Miraculous Though Not Virginal Birth

THE ACT TO WHICH men owe their lives is neither original nor miraculous. Yet the sacred legends often attribute a special significance to it and veil it in many cases in mystery.

There is no such thing as a virgin birth in the Old Testament. The misinterpretation of a Messiah-passage (Isa. VII: 14), so often quoted as the prophetic announcement of Christ by Catholic theologians, is now clearly recognized. The mistranslation of the Hebrew word "alma," which means a young woman of marriageable age, is, as Christian scholars have long admitted, responsible for the mistake that has been continued through so many centuries. The famous sentence does not say "Behold, a virgin will conceive," but "a young woman will conceive."

No, there is no such thing as a virginal conception told of the women of the Old Testament. But something similar or akin to it was several times reported, namely a miraculous though not virginal birth. Isaac, for instance, had as much difficulty in being born by his mother as in being slain by his father. He was almost sacrificed by Abraham and remained almost unborn by Sarah. Only luck carried him through in both cases. A miracle prevented him from being slain and a miracle had to happen to make his birth possible.

The Scriptures report that Abraham's wife bore him no children, but God promised him that Sarah would give him an heir and she would be a mother of nations. Abraham laughed and said in his heart "Shall a child be born unto him that is an hundred years old? and shall Sarah, that is ninety years old, bear?"

When the three men later appeared to him on the plains of Mamre, they also predicted that Sarah would

: 186 :

have a son. Sarah, listening at the tent door behind the speaker, "laughed within herself, saying, After I am waxed old, shall I have pleasure, my lord being old also? And the Lord said unto Abraham Wherefore did Sarah laugh, saying, Shall I of a surety bear a child, which am old? Is any thing too hard for the Lord? . . ." It is clear that the Lord censured Sarah's laughter with these words. The very human report continues: "Then Sarah denied, saying, I laughed not; for she was afraid. And He said, Nay; but thou didst laugh."

Here is almost a tiff from a Biblical *Symphonia Domestica*. Here a little family scene is presented, the climax of which is the question "Wherefore did Sarah laugh?" It is, of course, a rhetorical question in the mouth of the Lord, since He knows wherefore. Does He not know everything? Even we who are not omniscient can guess wherefore the woman laughed. Abraham was one hundred years old when his son Isaac was born to him, nine months after the announcement, and Sarah was not much younger. They were both "well stricken in age; and it ceased to be with Sarah after the manner of women" (Gen. XVIII: 11).

The reason why Sarah laughed can hardly be doubted, and we can only wonder why some commentators give such far-fetched explanations for it. Benno Jacob, for instance, writes of that situation in which Sarah hears the odd announcement as a "moment of overwhelming joy" (*Augenblick überquellender Freude*).[1] Since the words of the Genesis story are not ambiguous, such an interpretation amounts to the irreverent view that the Lord is a bad psychologist. Sarah's laughter is one of scorn and not of mirth, as are almost all laughters reported in the Old Testament. Schopenhauer's explanation of the general nature of that emotional outburst, according to which "the cause of laughter in every case is simply the sudden perception of the incongruity between a concept and the real objects which have been thought through in some relation," is here well applicable.[2]

Considering the ages of Abraham and Sarah, there is enough incongruity in the promise of the Lord to make the laughable transparent. The patriarch's wife laughed like someone who hears an incredible or ridiculous statement: she could not believe what she had heard. Yet she did not express her incredulity. The lady doth protest too little, methinks—therefore she laughs. Her guilt feeling and her denial that she has laughed clearly prove the character of her laughter.

Let me insert here a little vignette demonstrating the delicacy of feeling which the Lord shows on this occasion, according to a post-Biblical legend.[3] It is reported in that legend that God, regardful of the peace of the family, did not accurately repeat Sarah's disrespectful remarks about Abraham's impotence to the old patriarch. Abraham might have taken amiss what his wife had said about his advanced years. In the view of that legendary commentary, so precious is the peace between husband and wife that even the Holy One—blessed be He—preserved it at the expense of truth.

Another rabbinical legend tells of a minor miracle that was added to the inscrutable mystery of Isaac's birth. To silence those who significantly asked "Can one a hundred years old beget a son?", God commanded the angel who had charge of giving the embryo form and shape to fashion Isaac precisely to the image of Abraham, so that all seeing the baby might claim "Abraham begot Isaac."

The idea of perfect likeness appears also in legendary presentations of the stories of Abraham and Isaac which show quite a few astonishing analogies. We have already mentioned that father and son appear in some legends as doublets. The old saga motif of the attempted killing of the child by a king or another mythical father representative immediately after birth is not to be found in the Isaac story, but it is obvious in the post-Biblical sagas about Abraham's miraculous escape from certain death. In his *Legends of the Jews* Ginzberg has collected the cycle of stories dealing with Abraham's birth and early childhood. The legends of Abraham as a child have variations parallel to Ishmael's exposure in the desert as well as to Isaac's near sacrifice (Abraham in the fiery furnace, his body bound hand and foot).[4]

The Scriptures tell the story of the miraculous, but not virginal, impregnation of Sarah. The future birth of a son to her is announced by the angel Michael. The closest analogy to this myth is to be found in the Protevangelium of James, an apocryphal writing of the second century. In this legend Joachim and Anna had no children and their unfruitful union caused them to be exposed to public contempt. One day an angel appeared to Anna and said to her, "Anna, Anna, the Lord hath harkened to thy prayer; thou shalt conceive and bring forth a child and thy posterity shall be spoken of throughout the whole world." At the same moment Joachim, who was tending his flocks in the field, also received a revelation from heaven. An angel said to him, "Joachim, Joachim, the Lord hath harkened to thy prayer; descend hence for behold thy wife will conceive in her womb." We know that the marvelous events related in the Protevangelium herald the birth of Mary, the daughter of Joachim and Anna. Also this legend reports, as does the Abraham-Sarah saga, a miraculous though not virginal birth. Also the message of the future child delivered to the husband and the wife by an angel is similar to the one recounted in the Genesis narrative.

The Lore of the New Testament relates that Joachim had spent five months in the desert when the angel appeared to him. This angel of the saga reminds Joachim of other mothers in Israel's tradition whose womb was closed by God not as a punishment, but only to be opened later more marvelously. The angel who functions as messenger and history teacher says: "The first mother of Israel, Sarah, was barren until the ninetieth year of her life and then she gave birth to Isaac to whom the benediction of all people was promised. And the mother Rebecca was barren for twenty years before she gave birth to Esau and Jacob, called Israel. And the mother Rachel was childless for many years, until God gave her Joseph who saved the world from starvation. And who was stronger than Samson or holier than Samuel? Yet their mothers were barren for many years before they gave birth to their sons. Thus you may believe by example that the child that will be given you will be more marvelous."[5]

Then follows the announcement of a daughter to be called Mary.

These examples of miraculous births are described in the Scripture. Joachim could, of course, not anticipate that his still-unborn daughter could have an even more miraculous impregnation.

The Gospel of Matthew says: "Now the birth of Jesus Christ was on this wise: When as his mother Mary was espoused to Joseph, before they came together, she was "found with child of the Holy Ghost" (I:18). The Holy Ghost had entered Mary at the Annunciation and she had supplied the divine Jesus with a mortal body. In this view Jesus had become a spiritual son of the Lord.

The saga of virgin birth was by no means confined to the story of Jesus. Centuries before him the Egyptian Pharaoh was supposed to have been conceived by Rā, who secretly descended to earth and begot him by a mortal mother. From the XVIIIth dynasty on it was dogmatically believed that the god Amen fathered every Pharaoh. In order to visit the queen he took the appearance of the royal consort. Adonis had been born of the virgin Myrrha. Apollo was supposed to be the father of Julius Caesar and of Augustus. Jesus' immaculate birth was thus no novelty in the mythology of the ancient world.

From the superficial viewpoint there is a great distance between the miraculous birth of Isaac and the virginal birth of Jesus, announced by the angel. But at a more penetrating glance one can see it as only a short step. The concept of a miraculous birth, that is a supernatural birth, can only be interpreted as the result of a divine impregnation. But this means that the child was not fathered by the legal husband of the woman who gives birth to it, but by a god or a divine agent. Who would this agent be but God, who predicted that the miracle would come to pass? In other words, the son who will be born is the child of the god who performs the miracle of impregnation. Isaac who came to the world in this unusual way is thus to be recognized as the son of Yahweh. Abraham is, so to speak, the legitimate father, in the same manner as the carpenter Joseph is the father of Jesus of Nazareth.

Isaac's miraculous though not virginal birth comes as close to the idea of divine conception as possible in terms of the Old Testament. From the miracle of Isaac's conception by a very old couple, it is only a small step to the great event, the birth of the Redeemer, with which a new era began. Isaac is also in this sense the herald of that other cult hero, and the near sacrifice of Abraham's son is a prelude to the drama of Calvary.

CHAPTER XVII

They Call It the
Binding of Isaac

I N COMPARING the Isaac story with the Gospels we
only cautiously trod the same path the early church
fathers boldly and unflinchingly walked. They unhesitatingly claimed that Isaac was the precursor or rather
the harbinger of the Saviour and that his arrested sacrifice preformulated the death on the cross.

Judaism does not acknowledge the phrase "sacrifice of
Isaac," since the Genesis story tells of an attempted, but

averted, sacrifice. To term it a sacrifice would be like calling a planned but prevented murder a killing. When the Jewish theologians speak or write about that *cause célèbre* of the patriarchal time—and they speak and write about it frequently—they use the term "Akedah" which means "the binding." The expression refers, of course, to the verse of the twenty-second chapter of Genesis: "And Abraham built an altar . . . and bound Isaac his son." The Christian theologians assert that the binding of Isaac foreshadows the crucifixion of Jesus.

The significance attributed by the Jews to the Akedah is reflected in the frequent recitals of that story in the Jewish liturgy. In some places the chapter is read daily during the morning service, but in all Jewish communities the tale of Isaac's binding is recited with great solemnity on the Jewish New Year's Day.

The motivation for this practice becomes transparent when one considers that New Year's is believed to be the day of Judgment and heralds the day of Atonement that follows ten days later. On this occasion the Shofar is blown, the instrument made from the horn of the ram offered as a burnt offering in place of Isaac. When Rabbi Abbahu was asked why that ram's horn should be sounded, he explained that it was because God said "Sound before Me the ram's horn so that I may remember on your behalf the binding of Isaac, the son of Abraham, and account it to you as if you had bound yourself before me."[1] The sounding of the ram's horn is not just a mnemonic device addressed to the Lord. It is a reminder to Him of the treasury of merits, of the recompense due for the good deeds of great men.

Those merits have accumulated into a fund upon which Israel can draw when it has sinned. As long as the Lord remembers the Fathers He keeps the world in mind.[2] Of all the great deeds of the patriarchs, the Akedah of Isaac, that binding on the altar, was praised as the noblest. It forms one of the main themes of Jewish liturgy. Midrash Tankuma, Genesis, tells the story:

The Holy one, blessed be He, said to Abraham: "Abraham, you have said what you had to say. I will now say what I have to say. In the future, the children of Isaac will sin before Me and I will sit in judgment over them on Rosh Hashana. And if they wish Me to find merit in their behalf to recall for their sake the binding of Isaac, let them sound this horn before Me."

"What horn?" Abraham asked.
"Look behind you," God said to him.

Forthwith Abraham lifted up his eyes, and looked, and behold, behind him a ram caught in the thicket by its horns.

God is indeed reminded of that great event in the New Year's service in the following words: ". . . Remember in our behalf, O Lord our God, Thy covenant and Thine oath to our Father Abraham on Mount Moriah! May this scene rise in remembrance before Thee: Abraham our Father binding his son Isaac on the altar and suppressing his own compassionate feelings in order to do Thy will wholeheartedly. So may Thy wrath, through Thy great mercy, turn away from Thy people. . . ."

Philo of Alexandria devotes many pages to the great merits of Abraham, whose act appears to him as more distinguished and more exalted than other noble deeds of history. Also Josephus magnifies Abraham's greatness, his act was the more extraordinary since Isaac was an unusual lad who endeared himself to his parents "by the exercise of every virtue."[3] In never tiring eloquence the rabbis again and again exalted Abraham's deed and his willingness to sacrifice his only beloved son.

Very soon a new idea emerged in connection with Abraham's noble and loyal attitude.

In the trial scene of *The Merchant of Venice* Shakespeare's Portia calls mercy "an attribute to God himself," and men become like him "when mercy seasons justice."

> Therefore Jew,
> Though justice be thy plea, consider this,
> That in the course of justice none of us
> Should see salvation: we do pray for mercy,
> And that same prayer doth teach us all to render
> The deeds of mercy.

Two millennia before Portia's speech, a prayer for mercy exhorts God that just as Abraham did not hesitate to offer Isaac, so God should be lenient with Isaac's descendants. "When they fall unto sin and bad deeds, remember for their benefit the Akedah of Isaac, their father, and rise from the throne of justice to the throne of mercy and be filled with mercy for them and have pity on them, and change the quality of justice to the quality of mercy for their sake."

Among the early church fathers the Carthaginian Tertullian gave to the doctrine of good works an essentially juristic stamp, which is not astonishing since he was himself a jurist. He argues that Abraham served as a model for God. "Abraham whom his faith made obey the command of God offered his only, beloved son as sacrifice to God so that God in His part bestowed on him the favor of the redemption of his posterity."[4]

The Binding of Isaac not only became a central theme in Jewish liturgy, but also played a role in the service of the Church. The First Lesson on Good Friday in the Church of England is a recital of the Akedah, which is followed by a reading of the chapter of St. John XVIII reporting the beginning of the Golgotha events. The Catholic priest chants the tale of Isaac's binding at the altar on Holy Saturday. Then follows the prayer which begins, "Oh God, the Supreme Father of the faithful who throughout the world didst multiply the children of Thy promise . . . and by the paschal mystery dost make Abraham Thy servant the father of all nations."

When the priest extends his hands over the consecrated wafers in the Mass, he says, ". . . accept them, as Thou didst vouchsafe to accept the gift of Thy servant Abel and the sacrifice of our patriarch Abraham."

In consecrating an altar the priest prays that it may "have as much grace with Thee as that which Abraham, the father of faith, built when he was about to sacrifice his son as a figure of our redemption."[5]

The story of the Binding of Isaac became a symbol of Jewish martyrdom. It was recited by the Jews during the terrible horrors of their persecution during the Middle Ages. They conceived of the Akedah as an example of Jewish faithfulness and as a model of devotion. Many compositions of prominent medieval Jewish poets, as for instance those by Ibn Gabirol, Moses and Abraham Ibn Esra, and Kalonymus ben Judah, were called Akedahs and were composed in rhyme and acrostic.[6] In the story of Hanna and her seven sons the mother says to her martyred children, "Children, go and tell your father Abraham, 'You have bound one sacrifice on the altar. I, however, have erected seven altars.'" When Jewish fathers and mothers slew their own children during the persecution of the Crusades to save the children from baptism, the sacrifice they made was considered as meritorious as that of the patriarch Abraham.[7]

In post-Biblical times another aspect of the Akedah story became more and more prominent: not Abraham's but Isaac's merits were celebrated and praised. There is no indication for the presence of this factor in the Biblical narrative. It seems that it first emerged in the age of Apocryphal literature. The trend is evident in Josephus, who let Isaac say to Abraham that he was willing to be sacrificed. The Jewish literature of the following period increasingly demonstrated Isaac's merit. It made him appear older and therefore more responsible and mature. While Josephus wrote that Isaac was twenty-seven years old, some other authors said that he was thirty-seven when the sacrifice was planned.

In some legends he is not only willing but eager to be sacrificed. We remember that he resists the temptations of Satan, who wanted to prevent him from being used as a burnt offering. (Compare the temptations of Christ in the wilderness.) To heighten Isaac's merit, the events on Mount Moriah are presented in such a way that the sacrifice is not only proposed, but really performed. One rabbi said, "As soon as the sword touched Isaac's neck, his soul flew out and escaped. When God caused His voice to be heard from between the cherubim and said, 'Do not stretch forth thy hand to the youth,' his soul returned to his body." Isaac was thus considered dead and returned from the dead. The son did more than merely assist his father in preparing for his own slaughter. The father was glad to sacrifice, the son to be sacrificed. God was sitting and watching the father binding and the son being bound.

When God was angry at David's numbering of his troops and was about to destroy Israel, He saw Isaac's ashes and this sight led Him to spare His people. Berakhot 628 of the Babylonian Talmud explained that ashes were put on the head while fasting, to call God's attention to the ashes of Isaac.[8]

It seems thus that by-and-by Abraham's merit receded and Isaac's came to the front. In this development the way was paved for the son, who was now the leading figure, to become divine. His death was followed by resurrection. Yet it was not Isaac, but a late revenant, who succeeded in ascending to Heaven. In Christ's expiatory death the victim became the victor.

Isaac and Christ

THE STORY OF the Binding of Isaac consists of a succession of sufferings and is in this respect sometimes
compared with the Passion of Jesus. Some famous
pictures representing that Biblical narrative render it in a
sequence of scenes reminiscent of the Stations of the
Cross, for instance a painting by Bronzino which shows
six scenes, and another picture by Israhel van Meckenem
composed of five scenes.[1] In Paul's view the supreme
sacrifice of the Saviour takes the place of the near sacrifice
of Isaac. God takes the part of Abraham and Jesus that

of Isaac. Instead of the ram the Paschal lamb appears and its blood is shed.

The Binding of Isaac has, as Israel Levi puts it, *"une virtue expiatoire."*[2] This quality of the patriarch's sacrifice was transferred to the death on the cross (*"en même temps la virtue rédemptive au sacrifice d'Isaac passait à la mort du crucifix"*).

It is easy enough to discover in many of the post-Biblical stories and interpretations predecessors of the accounts of the Gospels. The figure of Isaac was early recognized as the prototype or prefiguration of Christ, or rather as one of a series of cult heroes whose last personification was the god who sacrificed himself at Golgotha.

Yet the resistance against acknowledging such a descent is still strong with Christian as well as with Jewish theologians. Benjamin Segal in his book *Moriah and Golgotha* quotes an essay by a German Protestant theologian, Arthur Brausewetter, who remembers that even in his schooldays the Isaac story was incomprehensible to him. I shall translate the most expressive of his sentences: "A father who goes to slaughter his only son at a lonely mountain-top, like a lamb-sacrifice . . . who without any question would have thrust the knife into his heart if in the last moment the liberating word of God had not reached his ear—here is one of the texts of the Old Testament against which all of our emotions and our

moral codes revolt—of all of them perhaps the most re-
pulsive (*"unter ihnen vielleicht der abstossendste"*).[3]
Brausewetter denies that there is any connection between
Isaac's arrested sacrifice and Jesus' death at Calvary, and
is only ready to conceive of the Isaac episode as a symbol,
"in a figure predicting a greater and more lasting sacrificial action of world history, namely the sacrifice of
Jesus, willed by God, on the cross of Golgotha."[4]

In contrast with such a determined denial, we remember Arnold Toynbee's comparison of the sacrifice
of the Moabite King's son, Abraham's interrupted slaughter of Isaac, and the self-sacrifice of Jesus of Nazareth. We
added a critical comment to this historian's unqualified
statement that all three actions were different expressions
of the same religious attitude. From a certain rarefied point
of view Toynbee is justified in comparing the three sacrificial acts. To the unbeliever they will appear as various
manifestations of a religious madness, whatever the
method in it may be. Each of them will make the historian of ideas wonder about the place of religion in the
evolution of civilization, and each of them will elicit
some embarrassing questions. Anatole France, following
some rambling thoughts, once expressed doubt that the
rabble of mankind was worth the Lord's sacrificing His
divine son for its redemption.

There are, however, some questions whose answers

are more rewarding for the historian interested in psychological research. For instance, what inner development led from the idea of Isaac's store of merit for his descendants to the notion of the redemption of all sinners through Christ? Not only the Biblical scholar but also the explorer of comparative religion asks what motivation, what religious and social factors are responsible for the shifting of the glory of the burnt offering from Abraham to Isaac. We have seen that in post-Biblical comments and folklore the attitude of Isaac became more and more exalted and his merits became more praised than those of Abraham whose faith and obedience had first held the center of attention. We could expect, as the result of this tendency, the development of a saga whose core would be a young hero, eager to be sacrificed, a figure very close to that rabbi from Nazareth.

Let us assume that a felicitous combination of scholarly investigation and imaginative sense would find an answer to the question why the merit for the sacrifice was shifted from Abraham to Isaac. Then another problem immediately arises, namely: Why did the emphasis of the merit not remain with Isaac? Why was it shifted and redirected to Abraham, the father, to whom is attributed the power and the glory in Judaism? Are there two emotional tendencies, operating in opposite directions? And what does this conflict between them mean?

There is no doubt that the later glorification of Isaac

was suppressed. The fight between those opposite tendencies was, however, renewed and revived. The glorified Isaac is followed by the deified Christ. The trial of the patriarch is continued in the Passion and redemptive Crucifixion on a similar mountain top two thousand years later.

The idea of an individual redeemer was alien to Judaism. Nearest to this Christian concept is the Saga of the Suffering Servant (Isa. LIII) whose suffering and death has an atoning value. But this is the utmost limit reached by Judaism. E. O. James points out that "to a Jew the idea of any one being at once a perfect sin-offering and at the same time an ideal high priest of the human race entering the heavenly sphere through his own blood to obtain redemption for mankind could be but the rankest blasphemy."[5] Why was the idea of mediation and of vicarious atonement, which became a cardinal doctrine of Christianity, never fully developed in Judaism?

At this point these and several other problems of great significance, generally neglected by the Biblical exegesis, loom before the searcher after truth. Far from thinking that I can guide the student on the often tortuous and intricate paths to the point of their solutions, I shall be gratified if I can make some suggestions about where a possible road to the solution of those problems can be found.

We return to the point of our departure because it rec-

ommends itself as the most advantageous position. We
discovered behind the Genesis saga traces of an older
tradition in which not the near sacrifice of Isaac, but his
initiation (including his alleged death and resurrection)
was the central theme. Puberty rites are generally periodically celebrated festivals in which many adolescents of
the same or similar age group are initiated and accepted
as adult members of the tribe. But there are not many
young men passing through the initiation rites on that
sacred mountain. There is a solitary single lad, Isaac, who
is sacrificed or, as we could not say, is killed and resurrected; who dies as an adolescent and is reborn as a man, as
an adult Hebrew.

The initiation or puberty rites underwent a long development from the neolithic phase in which they originated
to the time when the Hebrew tribes migrated from their
Arabic home to Babylonia and Canaan. I have sketched
this development in another book[6] and will, therefore,
present only its outcome. During many centuries of development from primitive puberty rites to the secret
societies and religious mysteries of antiquity, we have to
assume a phase in which the boys to be initiated had a
representative, a "universal novice," to use Henry A.
Bunker's good term.[7]

This divine or half-godlike figure was supposed to have
died and been resurrected. He served as a model with

whom the adolescents could identify, whose sufferings
and final triumph they shared. The divine-son gods of
the Near Eastern religions were perhaps originally such
figures of the "universal novice" and were only later
elevated to a higher rank. It is very likely that the cult
heroes of the "dream time," of whom the Australian
tribes speak, mark the beginning of that development.
Primitive puberty rites were now replaced by the initiation festivals of secret societies, some of which were
priestly societies.

In my book *Mystery on the Mountain* I endeavored to
show that the Hebrew tribes, who must have passed
through a similar phase, most energetically refused the
existence of such a "universal novice" and returned to
the more primitive form of initiation rites. But this later
phase of initiation was no longer restricted to boys at
puberty. It became extended to the whole people of
Israel. There was no secret initiation into a society of priests
as in Egypt. All the Israelites became a "nation of priests."
There was no longer any secrecy about that association.
The secret now concerned the nature of their god who
was incorporeal and whose name was unutterable.

Where is the place of a figure like Isaac in this development, and how does the Genesis saga fit into the picture?
I would conjecture that the Biblical story is a late elaboration of an older tradition and presents what is best called

an "abortive myth." This reassessment of the Isaac figure
and its saga results from the theory, fully discussed elsewhere, that there was once, in the religion of the early
Hebrews, a cult hero or divine son like Osiris, Attis and
Adonis who had been the subject of a primal tradition
dealing with his tragic fate and death which effected the
redemption of his worshipers.

I call that original Isaac saga an abortive myth because
it failed to develop fully and was arrested before it reached
its aim. This seems at first an arbitrary and too positive
statement. Abortive myth? Is the Genesis narrative not
an independent and well-rounded piece of fiction whose
dramatic character was often admitted and praised and
which is comparable to a novel with a surprise ending?
Yes, but we don't speak here of that tale as of a work of
composition, nor of its character as a result of the story
teller's craft, but of its place among the myths of the prehistoric Near East. That means of its position compared
with other sagas of the nomadic Hebrew tribes. The character of this myth is best recognized when you compare
it with other sagas, as you compare a child born prema-
turely with a child born at full term.

That incomplete or rudimentary myth must have dealt
with a son of God who committed the great crime against
the father-god and had to pay the supreme penalty. He
was not, as his late successor, Isaac, sacrificed to God, but

by God himself against whom he had revolted. After he had been cruelly punished and had died, he was resurrected.

The new religion of Yahwism introduced by Moses could not tolerate a son-god and tried to eradicate all memory of his existence. Yet it could not entirely obliterate the old tradition. It continued to live on, was reshaped and remodeled according to the new religious notions of Mosaism. Many essential features were repressed. Others were banned into the nether world of folklore, as, for instance, the death of Isaac on Mount Moriah and his resurrection. Isaac was made the willing victim of an intended sacrifice that was not performed. The idea of his death and resurrection, taken from the puberty rites and transferred to the figure of the "universal novice," was removed from official tradition.

Isaac's binding on the altar, as Christ's hanging on the cross, are variations of the same theme, of an old mythical *leitmotif*. It is a melody heard for many hundreds of years before it sounded in the time of Tiberius at Galilee. Franz Rosenzweig reminds us that "Prometheus had already been hanging from the rock for half a millennium before the Cross was lifted up at Golgotha."[8]

In *Mystery on the Mountain* I tried to show that the biography of the young Jesus follows the typical lines of a puberty initiation, that the motifs of his death and resurrection correspond to the death and rebirth in the initiation ritual of primitive societies. In a process of the "return of the repressed," the old myth, evolved from the puberty rites, re-emerged in the Passion, in the tale of the dying and the rising of the Christ figure.

An eminent French theologian, Maurice Goquel, has recently pointed out that Christianity is not the religion preached or taught by Jesus. Its content is "the drama of redemption accomplished by his death and resurrection. It depends therefore upon a sacred history culminating in the fact of resurrection." The creative source of Christianity was "the faith in the risen and glorified Jesus."[9]

The Christ story is a completed myth that reached its logical aim. It renewed the old idea and superstitions, resulting from the belief that the adolescent boys in primitive societies are killed during their initiation and then reborn.

The saga of Isaac was an early abortive myth of the Hebrew tribes. Isaac was, so to speak, a *"sauveur manqué."*

CHAPTER XIX

The Bar Mizvah
of Jesus

THE OBSERVANCE OF RITUALS and ceremonies is often
continued long after people have abandoned their
faith and the faith of their ancestors. Jews, who
have given up their religious allegiance for many years,
still attend the services on the High Holidays. Christians
who don't believe in Christ any longer visit the church at
Easter and Christmas. Religious rituals keep their hold on

many people who have long left the beliefs of their child-hood. Even certain commandments and ordinances that have been consciously brushed aside often maintain their unconscious emotional significance and influence the thoughts and mores of the unbelievers. Anatole France occasionally remarked that men make religions, but religions then make men, or at least shape them.[1] The impact of religious beliefs and dogmas is not so much dependent upon their content, their truth, or their symbolical meaning, as on the affection and admiration we, as children, felt for the persons who first conveyed them to us.

The mythological history of Christ or the report of the events of his life on earth, which shook the world a few hundred years after his death, appear to us as the reshaped narrative of a great prolonged initiation in theological garb, containing the fundamental features of death and resurrection, annihilation and rebirth. The Church still preaches Christ crucified and risen and coming again. Christianity has thus immortalized the puberty story of the divine novice who took the place of generations of adolescent initiates in the Australian bush.

Is there a corresponding mundane life of the boy Jesus, a biography of the carpenter's son before he became a Jewish migrant preacher? There is. It has only to be isolated, taken out of the context into which it was later put. It also has to be freed from the mythological cloak with which it has been enveloped, and to be understood in terms of the time and the Jewish environment in which the Galilean boy was born and bred.

It is not within the scope of this essay to deal with the so-called unknown part of Jesus' life reaching from his early boyhood to the time of his baptism by John. Even that period of his life which the theologians call "the hidden years" has been thoroughly studied and extensively examined. It is very likely that he played with other children and was in Nazareth his usual self which, unknown to others, was a very unusual self.

Only a single and special occasion from Jesus' apprenticeship years applies to our study. The Gospel according to St. Luke reports, after its prologue, that Mary brought forth her first-born son and wrapped him in swaddling clothes and laid him in the manger. Eight days after his birth he was circumcised and was brought to the temple for the redemption of the first born son according to the Law. Next it is reported that the child grew and waxed strong in spirit, filled with wisdom. Today we would say that the Jesus-child was a very intelligent boy and had a very high I-Q.

We hear nothing more about the boy until he reaches his twelfth year. That year, as every year, his parents went to Jerusalem, at the Feast of the Passover. Luke (II: 42-51) reports about this journey as follows: "And when they

had fulfilled the days, as they returned, the child Jesus
tarried behind in Jerusalem; and Joseph and his mother
knew not of it. But they, supposing him to have been
in the company, went a day's journey; and they sought
him among their kinsfolk and acquaintance. And when
they found him not, they turned back again to Jerusalem
seeking him. And it came to pass, that after three days
they found him in the temple, sitting in the midst of
the doctors, both hearing them and asking them questions.
And all that heard him were astonished at his understanding and answers. And when they saw him, they
were amazed: and his mother said unto him, Son, why
hast thou thus dealt with us? Behold, thy father and I
have sought thee sorrowing. And he said unto them, How
is it that ye sought me? wist ye not that I must be about
my Father's business? And they understood not the saying
which he spake unto them. And he went down with them,
and came to Nazareth. . . ."

The first part of this Passover story, the little unpleas-
antness within the carpenter's family, shows nothing extraordinary. An adolescent boy gets lost, not without
secret purpose. The worried parents ask relatives and ac-
quaintances, who perhaps answer "We haven't seen him
lately." The story takes its turn to the extraordinary at
the point when the searching parents find the boy in the
temple discussing learned subjects with the old and wise

men of the congregation. The remarkable aspect of the story is not only the place which the boy visits—other adolescents gone astray would certainly search for other localities—but also the part he plays there. This is certainly something to wonder about. Yet it is still nothing miraculous.

An especially gifted boy of twelve lecturing to his mathematics teacher in class might be considered a child prodigy, but from such an evaluation to the name of an incarnate god is a far cry. The parents who saw him sitting there in the midst of learned men both listening to them and asking them questions were, of course, amazed. The Gospel reports that all who heard him were astonished at the scope of his understanding.

Compare the situation with that of six-year-old Mozart playing at the court of the Austrian Empress. Is it not possible that the lad from Nazareth excelled himself in the synagogue for the glory of the Lord even as that boy from Salzburg did at Vienna *ad majorem Amadei gloriam?* Jesus' answer to their questions would be: Don't you know that I am concerned with the sacred things, with the Law and with God's will? Don't you know that I am a priest? My Father's business is, of course, the Jewish religion, the worship of God, here performed by His divine son.

Everyone familiar with Jewish religious custom will, on

reading St. Luke's description, think of Bar Mizvah. On this occasion the novice is called to recite a section of the Law in the synagogue, and he assumes the moral and religious obligations of an adult. In quite a few Jewish communities it is the custom that the Bar Mizvah boy is quizzed by the rabbi and is engaged in Talmudic disputation with the elders.[2]

Only a few changes to correspond with the extraordinary personality of Jesus are needed in order to recognize that Luke described the Bar Mizvah of the boy from Galilee.[3]

The carpenter's son and apprentice must have had some religious instruction and training while he grew up. According to Jewish tradition it was perhaps his father who first introduced him to the Torah ("And thou shalt teach them to the children") or, if the working man Joseph was not educated enough to teach the child, some rabbi at Nazareth instructed Jesus before he went to Jerusalem with his parents. He was perhaps taught the same things as any Jewish child of his age. A theologian recently expressed the view that except for that one incident recorded by Luke, "his boyhood was presumably like that of any other Nazareth boy."[4]

Luke, the "beloved physician" (Col. IV: 14), who wrote his report about the year 80 A.D., perhaps incorporated some oral tradition about Jesus' boyhood or had access to some unknown source during the two years he spent in Palestine. Samuel Sandmel assumes in his scholarly book that Luke may have heard something about the Jewish Bar Mizvah rite and thought that Jesus must have distinguished himself at this occasion.[5]

There is still some controversy among Biblical scholars as to whether the incident reported by Luke—and only by Luke—may be equated with the Bar Mizvah. Samuel Sandmel, for instance, declared that it is "neither a happy nor a correct" interpretation to conceive of the Gospel account in this way. He presents several arguments, for instance: That the Bar Mizvah celebration very probably did not exist at Jesus' time and is a later institution.[6] It was and is furthermore a ceremony for the synagogue, and not for the temple. Finally a youngster at Bar Mizvah exhibits his supposedly beginning maturity, while the narrative in Luke is a "legend of how a divine being was, as a wonderchild, intellectually more mature than the finest teacher."

I don't hestitate to assert that those three arguments are not conclusive. It is correct that the Bar Mizvah celebration does not appear in rabbinical writings before the 13th century, but to use the phrase of the famous French physician Jean Martin Charcot, this does not prevent it from existing (*"ca n'empêche pas d'exister"*). It could have been possible that this initiation celebration was a secret ritual whose public discussion was avoided.

Furthermore, the incident described in the Gospel of Luke need not have been the Bar Mizvah celebration as we know it today or even as it was known many hundreds of years ago. It was perhaps the forerunner to or a preform of the present ritual, with which it had only certain essential features in common.

The second argument, namely that Bar Mizvah is a ceremony of the synagogue and not of the temple is far from crushing. The Greek Gentile might easily have confused the two localities or not have taken their differences very seriously.

The third argument is, of course, easily refuted. The Gospel glorifies Jesus into a distinguished figure on this traditional occasion. Should we expect the young Jesus to behave at his initiation as any other adolescent? When the little Mozart played before the Austrian Empress Maria Thérèse, he was a child prodigy who overshadowed adult artists, but he performed at the same instrument and did essentially the same things as other pianists. The boy Jesus could well have astonished the doctors by his genius, yet Luke would still report his Bar Mizvah or a similar initiation ritual.

The essential issue is that Jesus underwent a kind of initiation. This is further confirmed by the separation from his mother, one of the typical features of the primitive puberty rites. In Jesus' statement that he is about his Father's business there is an echo of the transition of the adolescent from mother and sisters to the camp of the father and other adult men.

On another occasion later in his life Jesus turns determinedly away from his mother. The Gospel of St. Mark (III: 21-35) reports the scene in which the people tell Jesus that his mother and brothers stand outside calling him. "And he answered them, saying Who is my mother, or my brethren? And he looked round about on them which sat about him, and said, Behold my mother and my brethren! For whosoever shall do the will of God, the same is my brother, and my sister, and mother." Joseph Klausner remarks that Jesus here abruptly breaks the ties with his mother "with a brusqueness unlike the tenderness normally attributed to the Evangelist."[7] It is at all events significant that Jesus refuses to see his mother. Mary did not belong to the circle of his followers during his lifetime and joined the Christian community only after his death.

Drawing the line leading from the Isaac story to the scene in the temple reported by Luke, we see a continued development from the primitive initiation of the early Hebrew clans to a puberty ritual in the time of Jesus. This is apparent whether the Luke narrative describes a Bar Mizvah or another similar rite. The pith of the matter is that in the temple at Jerusalem, as on the sacred ground in the Australian bush, a ritual is performed by which a boy is changed into a man.[8]

Judaism and Christianity

WHILE BIBLICAL SCHOLARS see in the Isaac story a decisive and fundamental transition in the religious evolution of mankind, our analysis is, as the French would say, very *terre à terre*. In our attention to the tradition of ancient puberty rites we hear the echo of a savage tune from barbaric times, a tune later transposed into a minor key and transformed in its elaboration into a bucolic Canaanite theme.

: 223 :

Yet there is a genuine transition perceptible in the Genesis story, a change which was first referred to by Erich Wellisch. The young psychiatrist who died while his book *Isaac and Oedipus* was being printed in 1954, arrived at a re-evaluation of certain relationships and based his thesis on the exposition of the Biblical Isaac story. All human relationships, he points out, are modifications and extensions of the basic experiences within the family, especially of the relationships between parents and children. The way in which we behave towards our parents and children profoundly influences our personal life: "this decides, in the words of the Decalogue, whether or not the day will be long upon the land which the Lord our God giveth us."[1]

That fundamental relationships can, in Wellisch's view, be considered in three main stages: on the first and most primitive stage the father experiences aggressive tendencies, mainly toward his sons and especially toward his first-born son. In primitive societies this aggression leads to infanticide. The second stage is characterized by a reaction of guilt against those aggressive and possessive impulses. These opposing tendencies, affectionate feelings for the child versus the desire to exert full control over him, even to kill him, result in a compromise solution. But this compromise solution—the unconscious process known to us as the Oedipus Complex—leads to new emotional conflicts.

A kind of resolution of the Oedipus Complex can be reached when the possessive, aggressive and murderous emotions are almost entirely abandoned and replaced by loving and affectionate feelings between parents and children. But this third stage cannot fully reach its aim. The reason for this lies, in Wellisch's opinion, mainly in the fact that the Oedipus Complex is based on a Greek attitude to life. A re-evaluation of the Oedipus Complex and its resolution is, in the view of this analyst, facilitated by the study of the story of Isaac's arrested sacrifice. "In the Akedah experience the third stage of moral development of the parent-child relationship is reached in a completeness as in no other psychological experiences."[2]

It is unimaginable that with the interruption of Isaac's sacrifice—"the Akedah experience"—a new and entirely different attitude in the relationship between father and son suddenly entered the world, as this psychoanalyst asserts. All historical and psychological indications contradict such a venturesome assumption.

Emotional changes of such a deep kind do not occur abruptly. The ambivalent attitude of fathers to sons and of sons to fathers is a fateful and lasting one and can never be entirely obliterated. A "modification of instincts" such as Wellisch considers is a psychological impossibility. One can speak only of changes in the intensity of their mutual correlation. It is clear to us that primitive man and man of the Neolithic age had a much higher degree of ambivalence. With cultural progress and changes of living conditions, extreme emotional tension has diminished. It has not disappeared.

In reality only compromise solutions are possible between the opposing emotional tendencies in the relationship between fathers and sons. The fundamental conflict and contrast is not solvable. Needless to say, the Akedah experience presents only a partial and provisional adaptation.

It is, however, undeniable that the component of affection in the relationship of fathers and sons became stronger once it found expression in puberty rites. The outcome of the ritual was an awareness of the ties that joined the two generations together by vital necessities and tribal memories of a common past.

In his preface to my book, *The Ritual,* Freud summarized his reconstruction of the origins of religious life:[3] "God the father at one time walked incarnate on the earth and exercised his sovereignty as leader of the hordes of primitive men until his sons combined together and slew Him . . . the first social ties, the basic moral restrictions and the oldest form of religion—totemism—originated as a result of and a reaction against this liberating misdeed." Freud points out that later religions "are filled with the same content and with the endeavor to obliterate the traces of that crime or to expiate it by other solutions for the conflict between father and sons; while, on the other hand, they cannot refrain from repeating anew the removal of the father. As a result we can recognize the echo of that occurrence which throws its gigantic shadow over the whole development of mankind."

The events, beyond any memories, to which Freud here refers and which culminated in the killing and eating of the primal horde-father, form the frame into which theological interpretation a hundred thousand years later put the tradition of Adam's Fall.[4]

Other very faint echoes of the development of the earliest human society are heard in the Biblical myths. We recognize traces of a primal phase in which, hundreds of generations after that ancient crime, new family or clan organizations were again formed with father-figures at their head. There were perhaps expulsions of the rebellious sons after they grew up, as in the myth of Adam and Cain and perhaps even in the Joseph story. There was very likely a time in which the grown-up son who had to leave the camp had to search for women in distant tribes. Other incidents could be guessed at. During some period, perhaps, first-born sons were killed by their jealous fathers.

In a later development the adolescent males were subjected to the iron discipline of a tyrannical clan-father. Their rebellious tendencies were forcefully suppressed by the older men and they were allowed to remain within the clan only after they had been subjected to a brutal and cruel education consisting in bodily mutilations, punishments, curses and threats. The last development of these stern educational measures for the boys are the puberty rites found in all primitive societies.

In place of the totemistic ferocious monster or terrifying ghost of the Australian and African initiations, the Hebrew god dominates the scenes of the Biblical myths. Content with a ram as redemption for the boy who should have been slaughtered, he has now considerably mellowed, but he is still terrifying enough to enforce "unconditional surrender." The gigantic shadow that has been thrown over the development of mankind is no longer called Balum or Duramelin. He now has a secret name, later on replaced by the word Yahweh.

The attempts at solution of that age-old conflict between father and son continue in various forms. The conflict was not only a power-struggle. The prize of the fight was the possession of the women of the clan. Traces of those oldest conflicts are easily recognizable in all the myths of the ancient Near East. These traces also appear, though repeatedly changed and rechanged, in the myths of the Bible.[5]

Those myths are daydreams of young mankind, fulfillments of early wishes, often projected into the realm of gods or divine beings. Young son-gods such as Attis, Adonis, Osiris win the upper hand with the great mother-goddesses. But they have to atone for the reoccurring crime of having dispossessed and killed the powerful father-god. Their triumphs are short lived and they die a cruel death. They are eventually resurrected and take the position of the defeated old tyrant-father, whose divine power they sometimes share—the Kingdom of Heaven and of Earth.

In the essential features of the Biblical Isaac story and especially in the post-Biblical legends, we look for remnants of an early tradition telling of an uprising of the only son, of the suppression of his revolt and of the resulting punishment. A later manifestation of the same theme, especially of the atoning penalty, can be discovered in the figure of the suffering servant as conceived by Isaiah.[6] The attempts to break the power of the father-god were repeated but remained unsuccessful. They reached a climax in the myth of Christ as Paul envisioned and fashioned the tale of the Passion and Redemption.

Here again emerges the figure of a young son-god and rebel, who took the terrible punishment which not only repeated the primal crime of revolt but also freed sinful mankind. The sacrifice arrested in the case of Abraham's son was suffered by Christ. In it man and God who had been incarnated confessed to his old crime against the primal father and atoned for it.

It is at this point that Judaism and Christianity part ways. In the Old Testament there is an arrested sacrifice. In the New there is a supreme self-sacrifice brought to completion. In the Old Testament there is an only beloved son who almost became a god. In the New there is the Son of Man who is the incarnate deity.

In Christianity the son-God became victorious although he was the victim of his expiatory self-sacrifice. Judaism remained a father religion. The intense and revivified need to "Honor Thy Father," the heritage of conquered impatience and mastered rebelliousness, forms an unbroken tie through the generations of Israelite history. No one who has grown up in a Jewish family can escape its emotional hold. Whatever attempts had been made to introduce a son-figure like Tamuz, Osiris or Adonis, whom the neighboring people worshipped, were forcefully suppressed in Yahwism.

The supremacy of the father-god was maintained. In their stubbornness the Jews rejected not Jesus, the carpenter's son of Nazareth, but Christ, the only son of the Lord. They would acknowledge no salvation or atonement for the primal crime. There was no confession that such a crime was committed, nor any expiation for it as in the crucifixion of Christ. In their rejection of Christ, the Jews expressed their disbelief that the "universal novice" had died and was resurrected. It is as if they denied that there had been such a miracle, as if they knew better.

There are fundamental differences between Judaism and Christianity, especially in its Pauline form. Paul proclaimed certain views that have become authoritative Christian doctrines, of which the Jew Jesus knew nothing and which he would have determinedly rejected. This is not the place to discuss these fundamental differences of doctrines, for instance those of Original Sin, of the Trinity, of the Immaculate Conception and the Virgin Birth. The great divide remains the divine Sonship of Christ and the Atonement for all sins of humanity by his sacrificial death.

Christianity conquered the Western World and celebrated, without being aware of it, the victory of the son-god over his divine Creator. But Judaism was unaffected by this victory and remained loyal to the father. It continued to live as if it wanted to immortalize the father-god. In contrast to the Christian creed, professing the Holy Trinity, Judaism proclaims that there is only one God and He is the only One.

The basic difference between Christianity and Judaism has not changed since it was discussed and argued in hundreds of theological disputations in Medieval times. Heinrich Heine once sarcastically formulated this differ-

ence in the words of Rabbi Juda of Navarra in the disputation that took place in the Aula of Toledo, in the presence of King Pedro (1350-1369) and of his lovely wife
Doña Blanka. The rabbi answers the vehement arguments
of the Franciscan Friar José:

> "Unbekannt is mir der Gott
> Den ihr Christum pflegt zu nennen.
> Seine Jungfer Mutter gleichfalls
> Hab ich nicht die Ehr zu kennen.
>
> . . . .
>
> Ob die Juden ihn getötet
> Das ist schwer jetzt zu erkunden
> Da ja das Corpus delecti
> Schon am dritten Tag verschwunden.
> Dass er ein Verwandter sei
> Unsres Gottes ist nicht minder
> Zweifelhaft; so viel wir wissen
> Hat der letztre keine Kinder.[7]

> Quite unknown to me the God is
> Whom you call the Christ, good brother,
> Nor have I ever had the honor
> To have met his virgin mother
>
> . . . .
>
> That the Jews in truth destroyed him
> Rests upon your showing,
> Seeing the delecti corpus
> On the third day vanished wholly.

It is equally uncertain
Whether He was a connection
Of our God, who has no children
In, at least, our recollection.

Yahweh, it is true, had no children. Yet the rabbis' recollection does not reach far enough back. Not Yahweh, but his predecessor had a son who rebelled against his father and suffered the punishment of death for it.

In the evolution of Judaism almost every trace of such a rebellious son-god, who was united with his great mother and consort, was removed. Only very few recognizable memory traces, difficult to decipher, are preserved in the Biblical myths. One of them is in the Isaac tradition in which we discovered an unfinished and rudimentary primal saga. Isaac was not sacrificed, nor did he offer himself as a sacrifice, as Christ did. He was condemned to have a shadow existence, compared with the life of his father Abraham and of his son Jacob.

The sacred myths are not just stories to be believed. They are supposed to bring "glad tidings," to promise salvation and redemption. None of the religions has succeeded in solving the problem posed by the unalterable constitution of man and the condition of living on this little planet, nor that other problem of the conflict between individual drives and the demands of society.

Anatole France once complained that, as if we were not

burdened enough with irksome duties toward our fellow men, religion wants us also to fulfill duties toward God.[8] Neither the arrested sacrifice of Isaac nor the supreme self-sacrifice of Christ has changed the fundamental facts of the human condition. They could not redeem man from his predicament, nor resolve the dilemma inherent in his nature.

In the Jerusalem Talmud the Lord said of His worshippers: "I wish that they abandon me, but that they observe my commandments."[9] It is certain that the first part of this statement is on the way to fulfillment. Human nature being what it is, one very much doubts that the second part of God's wish will ever be realized.

Postlude: Journey's End

THE ORIGIN OF THE NILE was still, one hundred years ago, in Sir Harry Johnston's words, "the greatest secret after the discovery of America." The quest for the sources of the Nile (we remember that the ancient Egyptians worshipped the great river as a god) preoccupied the Greeks and Romans. Even after H. M. Stanley found the tributaries of Lake Victoria, the problem was not fully solved. The springs of the Old River could later be defined when Bauman, Ramsay and Kandt followed the Kagara to its sources.

In a way similar to these expeditions, we followed the religious and social organization of the ancient Hebrews from patriarchal times to its beginnings. We followed the puberty rites on their long way until they evolved into the Passion of the universal Novice and Saviour. We have understood how the primitive initiation of prehistoric societies introduced the adolescents into the lore and religion of their tribes and enforced on the boys the tribal codes they would have to observe as adult members of their community. All other education of men was to be shaped after the model of those early elementary and unwritten laws imposed on the adolescents in the sacred grounds.

As this voyage of discovery has now arrived at its provisional end, I can state as its main result the discovery that the prehistoric culture of the Jews was built on the superstructure of primitive initiation. It would perhaps be preferable to say that it was built on the enduring effects of that initiation, namely on the bond between the older men of the tribes and the newly accepted young men. This bond, sanctioned by the gods and later by Yahweh, formed a firm tie between the generations and a strong link in the chain of traditions. The social and religious life of the prehistoric Hebrews, originally set in a forgotten mould of a proto-ritual, hardened through many centuries. It is essentially the same image of a dark and dangerous deity who imposes the laws and it is the same ritual, reshaped and centered around death and resurrection, that determines the attitude of the young men admitted to the Jewish and Christian communities.

When, more than forty-six years ago, I first grappled with this idea, I tried to formulate its essence in a lecture at the Vienna Psychoanalytic Society, *The Puberty Rites of the Savages,* published shortly afterwards.[1] I could not then foresee that more than four decades later, I would return to the subject. I was not then aware that it had gotten hold of me and would not release me. The problem that had preoccupied me as a young psychoanalyst re-emerged in old age.

Freud, who bestowed the first prize for applied psychoanalysis on that early paper, often encouraged me to continue my research in this direction, but I had turned my attention to other psychoanalytic problems. I now understand what prevented me then from completing those attempts at investigation. In his *Pensées,* Nicolas Chamfort (1741-1794) called conviction "the conscience of the mind." Also this form of conscience sometimes "doth make cowards of us all." It needs moral courage to take the risk of failure. To be convinced is not enough. One has to have the courage of one's conviction and freely express it. It seems that I acquired this moral courage only in old age.

This book is the fourth in a series of explorations in which I have tried to penetrate with psychoanalytic methods the core of Israel's prehistory. Investigating the myths and early traditions of the prehistoric Hebrews, I first attempted to disentangle the historic facts from the fantasies in the Biblical saga of the Fall of Man.[2] In another book on the creation of woman I could demonstrate the hidden connections of the Biblical myths with the essential features of Semitic puberty rites.[3] The fundamental revelation on Mount Sinai, dealt with in a third book, appeared to me as a tradition in whose core the secret of a great initiation festival of Hebrew tribes is fused with recollections of the Exodus from Egypt.[4] The final essay, presented here, endeavors to fill the gap that is formed by our lack of understanding of some patriarchal traditions. This tetralogy presents the prologue and the first act of the drama of Jewish destiny. As in individual life, the earliest phase of a people's history forms its most important part and determines its later development.

With this exploration we have arrived at the dawn of Israel's entrance into the world of the ancient Near East. At these frontier lines we have reached the end of this expedition of discovery. Looking back at its results, I hope that I have imparted a cohesive and meaningful picture, however marred by blots and blemishes, of prehistoric Israel.

It has been my good luck (and nothing but this) to have discovered some secrets concealed in the traditions of the Hebrew tribes. In following those traces I was mindful of Freud's advice that one should listen to one's self-critical voices very acutely, and to those of others with some attention. I hope that I have learned from him to look unflinchingly at surprising phenomena, to pursue knowledge patiently wherever it may lead; and I hope that I have acquired some of that "defiant courage of truth" of which he spoke in a letter of 1929. As a minority of one I was prepared to face the doubts and criticisms of the experts and to qualify my statements whenever they were corrected. I thought that the Biblical scholars would after a longer period of reassessment hesitatingly acknowledge the significance of my contributions.

I was not prepared for the assault and abuse from Christian and Jewish theologians, believers and non-believers. The vehemence and bitterness of criticism I had incurred by the reconstruction of an unknown past surprised me. A few of my other books had been read by so many people that I have sometimes been overwhelmed by fame; but I have also become known as the infamous author of "some books on Hebrew origins." The results of my research were treated as though tracing the most valuable achievements of Jewish culture to crude and primitive beginnings amounted to their downgrading and degradation.

: 239 :

Even the reproach of Jewish self-hate, once ridiculously flung at Freud, was again picked out from the arsenal of old weapons. I had attributed a certain value to the results of my research, but it was modest. I am tempted to quote a fine sentence of Voltaire's, who once complained that the sharpness of the attacks upon him transgressed by far his merits. (*"J'ai été persécuté fort au delà de mon mérite."*)

In spite of the majority of negative reactions to the fundamental and far reaching conclusions presented in my three books which form, together with the present one, a Biblical tetralogy, I am sure that the initiation rites will be recognized as the backbone of the religious and social culture of ancient Israel. Being seventy-three years old, I cannot hope to see the acknowledgement of my theories, but I am bold enough to predict that the stone which the builders refused will become the cornerstone of an important body of knowledge. I am painfully aware of the shortcomings, gaps and inevitable mistakes in this reconstruction of a prehistoric past. But the sense of urgency prevails. I offer the results of my work and investigation in the spirit of inquiry, with the expectation that others will continue to build upon the structure here begun.

References

PRELUDE: *The Beginning*

1. Theodor Reik, *The Ritual* (Vienna and Leipzig: Psycho-analytischer Verlag, 1919; New York: International Universities Press, 1958).
2. —— *Myth and Guilt* (New York: George Braziller, 1957).
—— *Mystery on the Mountain* (New York: Harper & Brothers, 1958).
—— *The Creation of Woman* (New York: George Braziller, 1960).

PART ONE: THE CHALLENGE OF THE PROBLEM

CHAPTER 1. *Prologue*

1. Heinrich Heine, "Hebrew Melodies," trans. by Margaret Armour, *Prose and Poetry* (New York: E. P. Dutton, 1934).

2. Solomon Goldman, *Book of Human Destiny, In the Beginning* (New York: Harper & Brothers, 1949), p. XI.

CHAPTER II. *On The Fringes of the Saga*

I shall not burden this chapter with footnotes giving the precise quotations of every passage. Readers interested in the sources will easily find them in the following books:

B. Beer, *Das Leben Abrahams nach Auffassung der jüdischen Sage* (Leipzig: O. Leinen, 1859).

Louis Ginzberg, *Legends of the Jews* (Philadelphia: Jewish Publication Society, 1911 ff.).

Joseph ben-Gurion, *Die Sagen der Juden* (Frankfurt a.M.: Rutten und Loening, 1919).

Joseph Goer, *The Lore of the Old Testatment* (Boston: Little, Brown & Co., 1951).

Solomon Goldman, *Book of Human Destiny, In the Beginning, op. cit.*

CHAPTER III. *The Comments of Theologians and Exegetists*

1. Solomon Goldman, *Book of Human Destiny, In the Beginning, op. cit.*, p. 793.
2. H. Gollancz, "The Sacrifice of Isaac," *The Imperial and Asiatic Quarterly Review,* January-April 1895, New Series, Vol. XI, p. 139.
3. John Skinner, *A Critical and Exegetical Commentary on Genesis* (New York: Charles Scribner's Sons, 1925), p. 528.

4. Dorothy B. Hill, *Abraham, His Heritage and Ours* (Boston: Beacon Press, 1917), p. 176.

5. Julian Morgenstern, *A Jewish Interpretation of the Book of Genesis* (Cincinnati: Union of American Hebrew Congregations, 1958), p. 158.

6. Tan Toledot 57 f 40 a, quoted from G. Montefiore and A. Loewe, ed., *A Rabbinic Anthology* (Philadelphia: Jewish Publication Society, 1960), p. 303.

7. Eduard Stucken, *Astralmythen,* (Leipzig: E. Pfeiffer & Co., 1896-1897).

8. Hugo Winckler, *Geschichte Israels,* (Leipzig: E. Pfeiffer & Co., 1900); —— *Altorientalische Forschungen III,* (Leipzig: E. Pfeiffer & Co., 1902).

9. Ignaz Goldziher, *Mythology among the Hebrews* (London: Longmans, Green & Co., 1877).

10. *Interpreter's Bible* (New York and Nashville: Abingdon-Cokesbury Press, 1952), Vol. I, p. 642.

11. Lawther Clarke, *Concise Bible Commentary* (New York: The Macmillan Company, 1950), p. 349.

12. Benno Jacob, *Das erste Buch der Tora, Genesis* (Berlin: Schocken Verlag, 1934), p. 500.

13. Otto Proksch, *Die Genesis* (2nd ed.; Leipzig, 1924), p. 316.

CHAPTER IV. *The Anthropological and Archaeological Approach*

1. Plutarch, "De Superstitione," quoted from James G. Frazer, *The Golden Bough* (New York: St. Martin's Press, 1955; London: Macmillan & Co., 1930), Part III, "The Dying God."

2. *Ibid.*

3. Porphyrius, *De Abstentia.*

4. Winckler, *Geschichte Israels, op. cit.,* Vol. II, p. 45. "Alles, was von Isaac erzählt wird ist Wiederholung der Abraham Legenden." ("All that is told of Isaac is a repetition of the legends of Abraham.")

5. Eduard Meyer, *Die Israeliten* (Halle: M. Niemeyer, 1906), p. 249 ff.

6. Jacobus and Zenos, ed., *New Standard Bible Dictionary* (New York and London: Funk & Wagnalls, 1920), p. 370.

7. James Hastings, *Dictionary of the Bible* (New York: Charles Scribner's Sons, 1927), Vol. II, p. 543.

8. E. O. James, *Myth and Ritual in the Ancient Near East* (New York: Frederick A. Praeger, 1958; London: Thames & Hudson, 1958), pp. 304–305.

9. Salo Wittmayer Baron, *Social and Religious History of the Jews* (Philadelphia: Jewish Publication Society; New York: Columbia University Press, 1952), Vol. I, p. 34.

10. O. Jeremias, *Abraham, Recent Discoveries and Hebrew Origins* (London, 1936), p. 76.

11. Yehezkel Kaufman, *History of the Religion of Israel* (Chicago: University of Chicago Press, 1960), pp. 221–222.

12. Sir Leonard Woolley, *The Royal Cemetery* (Philadelphia: University Museum, 1934), Vol. II, p. 87.

13. Harold H. Rowley, *The Changing Pattern of Old Testament Studies* (London: Epworth Press, 1959), p. 7, u. 8.

14. Peter Ustinov, *Diplomats* (New York: Bernard Geis Associates, 1960).

CHAPTER V. *The Existential Concept of the Myth*

1. *Interpreter's Bible, loc. cit.*
2. Sören Kierkegaard, *Fear and Trembling,* trans. with Introduction and Notes by Walter Lowrie (Princeton: Princeton University Press, 1954), p. 52.
3. Walter Lowrie, *A Short Life of Kierkegaard* (Princeton: Princeton University Press, 1944), p. 52. Compare the recent psychoanalytic paper by Edith Weigert, "Sören Kierkegaard's Moodswings," *International Journal of Psychoanalysis,* July–October 1960, pp. 531 ff.
4. Jean-Paul Sartre, *L'existentialisme est un humanisme* (Paris: Les Editions Nagel, 1946), p. 29.
5. Ignaz Maybaum, lecture on "The Sacrifice of Isaac, A Jewish Commentary," given in London, 1959.
6. Benjamin Segal, *Morija und Golgatha* (Berlin, 1915).

CHAPTER VI. *Psychoanalytic Interpretations*

1. Eduard Stucken, *Astralmythen, op. cit.*
2. Otto Rank, *Das Incestmotiv* (2nd ed.; Leipzig and Vienna: Psychoanalytischer Verlag, 1926), p. 307.
3. Dorothy F. Zeligs, "Abraham and Monotheism," in *American Imago,* 1953, No. 3, p. 313. Other notable psychoanalytic contributions by Dorothy F. Zeligs to the problem are "The Role of the Mother in the Development of Hebraic Monotheism" in *Psychoanalytic Study of Society,* 1960, p. 287; and "Abraham and the Covenant of the Pieces" in *American Imago,* 1961.

4. Roger E. Money-Kyrle, *The Meaning of Sacrifice* (London: International Psychoanalytic Library, 1930), p. 234.

5. Erich Wellisch, *Isaac and Oedipus, A Study in Biblical Psychology* (New York: The Humanities Press, 1954), p. vii.

6. *Ibid.*, p. 5.

7. *Ibid.*, pp. 5 and 116.

8. *Ibid.*, p. 93.

CHAPTER VII. *On Second Consideration*

1. Ludwig Jekels, "The Problem of the Duplicate Expression of Psychic Themes and Instinct Dualism in Dreams," *Selected Papers* (New York: International Universities Press, 1953), pp. 131 and 160.

2. Carl Heinrich Cornill, *History of the People of Israel,* trans. by W. H. Carruth (Chicago: Open Court Publishing Co., 1911), p. 29.

3. Article on Isaac by Hugo Fuchs in *The Universal Jewish Encyclopedia* (New York and London: Funk & Wagnalls, 1902–1906), Vol. V, p. 580.

4. A. E. Crawley, "On Human Sacrifice," *Encyclopedia of Religion and Ethics,* ed. by James Hastings (New York: Charles Scribner's Sons, 1908), Vol. VI, p. 840.

5. *Encyclopaedia Britannica* (1960 edition), Vol. IX, p. 803.

6. Yehezkel Kaufman, *History of the Religion of Israel, op. cit.,* p. 431.

7. E. O. James, *Origins of Sacrifice* (London, 1938), p. 25.

8. The idea connected with the expression "Abraham's Bosom," used in the parable of Dives and Lazarus (Luke XVI: 22, 23) may be considered as indication of a development in the direction of Abraham's deification. See

W. Winterbotham, "The Culture of Father Abraham," *Expositor*, 1896, Vol. II, pp. 177–186.

9. Otto von Kotzebue, *Voyage and Discovery*, English translation (London, 1821), Vol. III, p. 248.

PART TWO: THE SEARCH FOR A SOLUTION

CHAPTER VIII. *Smoke Screen Around a Burnt Offering*

1. Mary Ellen Chase, *Life and Language in the Old Testament* (New York: W. W. Norton, 1955), p. 116.

CHAPTER IX. *Death and Resurrection in the Puberty Rites*

1. Arnold van Gennep, *Les Rites de Passage* (Paris: E. Nourry, 1909). English edition (Chicago: University of Chicago Press, 1959).

2. D. F. Thompson, "The Hero Cult: Initiation and Totemism on Cape York," *Journal of the Royal Anthropological Institute*, 1933, p. 474.

3. James G. Frazer, *The Golden Bough* (3rd ed.; London: Macmillan & Co., 1913), Vol. II, p. 227.

4. *Ibid.*, p. 249.

5. Richard Neuhaus, *Deutsch New Guinea* (Berlin: J. Baer & Co., 1911), Vol. III, p. 402.

6. Richard Neuhaus, *op. cit.*, p. 418.

7. Carl Strehlow, *Das sociale Leben der Arand und Loritjastämme* (Frankfurt a. M., n. d.), p. 10.

8. Gunther Tessman, *Die Pangwe* (Berlin: E. Wasmuth, 1913), Vol. II, pp. 39–94.

9. James G. Frazer, *The Belief in Immortality and the Wor-*

ship of the Dead (London: Macmillan & Co., 1913), Vol. I, p. 230.

10. Louis H. Gray, *Encyclopedia of Religion and Ethics,* ed. by James Hastings, *op. cit.,* Vol. III, p. 667.
11. G. A. Barton, *Semitic Origins* (London, 1902), pp. 90, 100.
12. M. J. Lagrange, *Etudes sur les religions sémitiques* (Paris, 1903), p. 72.
13. Mircea Eliade, *Birth and Rebirth* (New York: Harper & Brothers, 1958), p. 23.
14. H. Straube, *Die Tierverkleidungen der afrikanischen Naturvölker* (Wiesbaden, 1955), pp. 8 ff.
15. Julius E. Lips, *The Origin of Things* (New York: A. A. Wayne, 1956), p. 168.
16. James G. Frazer, *The Belief in Immortality and the Worship of the Dead, op. cit.,* p. 260.

CHAPTER X. *Reconstruction*

1. Theophile James Meek, *Hebrew Origins* (New York: Harper Torchbooks, 1960), p. 83.
2. James G. Frazer, *Folklore of the Old Testament,* abridged edition (New York: The Macmillan Company, 1927), p. ix.
3. Mircea Eliade, *Birth and Rebirth, op. cit.,* p. xi.
4. Jean-Jacques Bernard, *Mon Père Tristan Bernard* (Paris: Albin Michel, 1955), p. 150.
5. Adolphe Lods, *Israel from the Beginnings to the Middle of the Eighth Century* (London: Kegan Paul, Trench, Trubner & Co., 1932), p. 200.
6. Compare Ishmael's circumcision as reported in Genesis XVII: 25. The word "bridegroom" (hathan) means a

circumcised man; the term for father-in-law (hothan) means "he who circumcised." W. Robertson Smith, *The Religion of the Semites* (New York: Meridian Books, 1956), p. 330.

CHAPTER XII. *The Covenant*

1. For the interpretation of that deep sleep in Biblical legends see my book, *The Creation of Woman, op. cit.,* p. 96.
2. W. Koppers, *Primitive Man and His World Picture* (London: Sheed & Ward, 1952), p. 140.
3. William J. Goode, *Religion Among the Primitives* (Glencoe, Ill.: The Free Press, 1951), p. 100.
4. W. Robertson Smith, *The Religion of the Semites, op. cit.,* Lecture IV, especially pp. 318 ff.
5. James G. Frazer, *Folklore of the Old Testament, op. cit.* pp. 153 ff.
6. For instance, John Murray, *The Covenant of Grace* (London: Tyndale Press, 1954).
7. Géza Róheim, "The Covenant of Abraham," *International Journal of Psychoanalysis,* Vol. XX, 1939.
   Arthur A. Brenner, "The Covenant with Abraham," *Psychoanalytic Review,* Vol. III, 1952.
8. W. Robertson Smith, *op. cit.,* p. 313.
9. Compare Mircea Eliade, *Birth and Rebirth, op. cit.,* p. 27.
10. A. W. Howitt, *The Native Tribes of Southeast Australia* (London: Macmillan & Co., 1954).
11. Mircea Eliade, *op. cit.,* p. 27.
12. Spencer and Gillen, *The Northern Tribes of Central Australia* (London: Macmillan & Co., 1904), p. 363.
13. *Mystery on the Mountain, op. cit.*

CHAPTER XIII. *Interchangeable Figures*

1. John Bright, *Early Israel in Recent History Writing* (Naperville, Illinois: Alec R. Allenson, 1956), p. 14.
2. *Ibid.,* p. 48.
3. John P. Peters, *Early Hebrew Story* (New York: G. P. Putnam's, 1904), p. 114 f.
4. Adolphe Lods, *Israel from the Beginnings to the Middle of the Eighth Century, op. cit.,* p. 19.
5. *Ibid.,* p. 15.
6. Martin Noth, *The History of Israel* (2nd ed.; London: A. C. Black, 1960), p. 120 ff. (New York: Harper & Brothers, 1958).
7. Martin Noth, *Ueberlieferungsgeschichte des Pentateuchs* (Halle: M. Niemeyer, 1945), p. 122.
8. Martin Noth, *op. cit.,* p. 122.
9. "Freud and the Future," speech delivered by Thomas Mann in Vienna, May 9, 1936, in celebration of Freud's eightieth birthday; published in Thomas Mann, *Essays of Three Decades;* here quoted from *Art and Psychoanalysis,* ed. by William Phillips (New York: Criterion Books, 1957), p. 369.
10. W. Robertson Smith, *The Religion of the Semites, op. cit.,* p. 18.
11. James G. Frazer, *The Golden Bough,* Vol. II, p. 246.
12. There are a few exceptions, for instance the excellent monograph by William Simpson, *The Jonah Legend* (London: G. Richards, 1899).
13. Theodor Reik, *Dogma and Compulsion* (New York: International Universities Press, 1931), p. 14.

14. George Gissing, *The Private Papers of Henry Ryecroft* (New York: E. P. Dutton & Co., 1903), p. 172.

CHAPTER XIV. *Hebrew Origins and Initiation Rites*

1. November 6, 1960.
2. W. Stanley in the article on the Bible in *Encyclopedia of Religion and Ethics, op. cit.,* Vol. II, p. 563.
3. *Mystery on the Mountain, op. cit.*
4. Baldwin Spencer, *Native Tribes of the Northern Territory of Australia* (London: Macmillan & Co., 1914), p. 91 ff, 115 ff, 121 ff, 153 ff. Compare the discussion of the subject in Mircea Eliade's *Birth and Rebirth, op. cit.,* p. 139.
5. *Ibid.*

PART THREE: FROM ISAAC TO JESUS

CHAPTER XV. *Moriah and Golgotha*

1. Joshua Adler, *Philosophy of Judaism* (New York: Philosophical Library, 1960), p. 136.
2. Dr. Julius Mark at Temple Emanu-El. Reported in the *New York Times,* November 20, 1960.
3. Asher, *Selichoth, The Daily Morning Prayers* (London: P. Vallentine, 1866).
4. Erich Wellisch, *Isaac and Oedipus, op. cit.,* p. 68.
5. *St. Cyril of Alexandria; A Library of Fathers of the Holy Catholic Church* (Oxford: J. H. Parker & Co., 1881).

6. *St. Athanasius: The Festal Epistles* (Oxford: J. H. Parker & Co., 1844).
7. Erich Wellisch, *op. cit.,* p. 72.
8. Israel Levi, "Le Sacrifice d'Isaac et la Mort de Jésus," *Revue des Etudes Juives,* Vol. LXIV, No. 128 (Oct. 1912), p. 181.
9. Louis Ginzberg, *Legends of the Jews, op. cit.,* Vol. VI, p. 254.
10. Arnold Toynbee, *A Historian's Approach to Religion* (New York and London: Oxford University Press, 1956).

CHAPTER XVI. *Miraculous but not Virginal Birth*

1. Benno Jacob, *Das erste Buch der Thora, Genesis* (Berlin, 1934), p. 428.
2. Arthur Schopenhauer, *The World as Will and Idea,* trans. by Haldane and Kemp (Colorado: Falcon's Wing Press, 1958), Vol. I, p. 76.
3. Louis Ginzberg, *Legends of the Jews, op. cit.,* Vol. I, p. 262.
4. *Ibid.*
5. Joseph Gaer, *The Lore of the New Testament* (Boston: Little, Brown & Co., 1952), p. 18.

CHAPTER XVII. *They Call It the Binding of Isaac*

1. Babylonian Talmud, Rosh Hashana 16 a.
2. This and the following references and quotations are taken from Efraim Frisch, *Zechuth Aboth and the Akedah,* reprinted from *Union College Annual,* pp. 253–266.

3. Flavius Josephus, *Antiquities,* I, 13.
4. Tertullian, *Adversus Judaeos,* 10.
5. C. G. Herbemann, ed., *The Catholic Encyclopedia* (New York: Robert Appleton Co., 1907), Vol. I.
6. For the history of the Akedah compare L. Zuns, *Die Synagoge Poesie des Mittelalters* (Berlin: J. Springer, 1955), pp. 13 ff.; I. Elbogen, *Der Jüdische Gottesdienst* (Leipzig: G. Fock, 1931), pp. 229, 433; and A. Z. Idelsohn, *Jewish Liturgy* (New York: Henry Holt & Co., 1932), pp. 44 and 236.
7. J. E. Fison, *The Faith of the Bible* (London: Penguin Books, 1957), p. 139.
8. Pirke Rabbi Eliezer, *Babylonian Talmud,* Berakhot 47 b.

CHAPTER XVIII. *Isaac and Christ*

1. Erich Wellisch, *Isaac and Oedipus, op. cit.,* p. 85. Wellisch gives a detailed iconography of the Akedah, p. 73.
2. Israel Levi, *Le Sacrifice d'Isaac et la Mort de Jésus, op. cit.,* p. 170.
3. Benjamin Segal, *Morija und Golgatha, op. cit.,* p. 73.
4. *Ibid.,* p. 8.
5. E. O. James, *Origins of Sacrifice, op. cit.,* p. 207. A. Dillman deals with the problem of vicarious atonement in his *Handbuch der alttestamentlichen Theologie* (Leipzig: S. Hirzel, 1895), p. 413 ff.
6. *Mystery on the Mountain, op. cit.,* pp. 175 ff.
7. Henry A. Bunker, "Psychoanalysis and the Study of Religion," *Psychoanalysis and the Social Studies* (New York, 1951), Vol. III, p. 28.
8. Franz Rosenzweig, *Stern der Erlösung* (Star of Redemp-

tion) (Leipzig: Felix Meiner Verlag, 1933), Vol. III, p. 150.

9. Maurice Goquel, *La Naissance du Christianisme* (Paris: Payot, 1946). English translation, *The Birth of Christianity* (New York, 1954), pp. 5, 20.

CHAPTER XIX. *The Bar Mizvah of Jesus*

1. "Les hommes font les religions et les religions font les hommes, ou du moins les forment." Michel Corday, *Dernières Pages inédites d'Anatole France* (Paris: Flammarion, 1927), p. 57.

2. Samuel Sandmel, *A Jewish Understanding of the New Testament* (Cincinnati: Hebrew Union College Press, 1956), p. 175.

3. Jacob A. Arlow, "Bar Mizvah. A Psychoanalytic Study of a Religious Initiation Rite," *Psychoanalytic Study of the Child,* edited by Ruth S. Eisler (New York: International Universities Press, 1951), Vol. IV, p. 358.

4. Joseph Klausner, *Jesus of Nazareth* (New York: Macmillan Co., 1927), p. 238.

5. Samuel Sandmel, *loc. cit.*

6. Leopold Loew, *Die Lebensalter in der jüdischen Literatur* (Szegedin, 1875) assumes that the fourteenth century is the date of the origin of the Bar Mizvah ritual. Compare also D. W. Wise, *Bar Mizvah and Confirmation in the Light of History and Religious Practice* (Cincinnati, 1933); and S. Schechter, *Studies in Judaism* (Philadelphia: Jewish Publication Society, 1924).

7. Joseph Klausner, *op. cit.,* p. 280.

8. It is a significant proof of the tenacity of the old rituals

that the youth is called "the Bar Mizvah groom." As
Jacob Arlow (in his paper mentioned before) points out,
this title is not accidental. It reflects the fact that in
primitive societies a young man can marry after having
passed the tribal initiation, while in our culture pattern
a boy of thirteen years does not marry.

CHAPTER XX. *Judaism and Christianity*

1. Erich Wellisch, *Isaac and Oedipus, op. cit.,* p. 3.
2. *Ibid.,* p. 4.
3. Theodor Reik, *The Ritual,* published in German in 1915.
American edition (New York: International Universities
Press, 1958).
4. See *Myth and Guilt, op. cit.*
5. See Dorothy Zeligs, "The Role of the Mother in the Development of Hebraic Monotheism," *op. cit.*
6. I shall not attempt to evaluate the role of Isaiah's figure
of the suffering servant as the model for the life and death
of Jesus. Hare Benzin, in *King and Messiah* (English
translation, London, 1955, p. 48), says: "We can state
historically that Jesus of Nazareth must have considered
Isaiah 53 the programme of his life and that he found
God's plan considering himself in these Old Testament
words."
7. Heinrich Heine, "Disputation," from *Hebraische Mel-
odieen,* Samtliche Werke, ed. by Otto F. Lachmann (Leipzig, 1887), Vol. I, p. 490. (The lines here quoted were
translated by my daughter Miriam Reik.)
8. Anatole France expressed this attitude several times, for
instance in his conversations with Michel Corday, *Anatole*

France, d'après ses confidences et ses souvenirs (Paris: Flammarion, 1927), p. 191: "Nous avons déjà bien des devoirs. Pourquoi avoir imaginé les devoirs envers Dieu qui n'existe pas?"

9. Jerusalem Talmud, Hagiga: 76, 3, p. 108.

POSTLUDE: *Journey's End*

1. "The Puberty Rites of Savages," read before the Vienna Psychoanalytic Society in January 1915; published in the journal *Imago*, Vol. IV, 1915–16, and in my book *The Ritual, op. cit.* In this paper it was pointed out that "in the sagas of the ancient Semitic people the same displacement onto gods who demand circumcision takes place. Among the Jews this command comes from Yahweh; the patriarchs (Abraham and Joshua) carry it out as representatives of the father. Australian rites derive the institution of circumcision (and subincision) from godlike beings, just as in the Jewish myths. The operation was introduced by the Mangarkunjerkunja who formed human beings in the primeval period; when it fell into disuse, or was carried out badly, two hawk-men came from the north and performed the circumcision with a stone knife on the men dwelling in the south . . . ," p. 111.

2. *Myth and Guilt, op. cit.*

3. *The Creation of Woman, op. cit.*

4. *Mystery on the Mountain, op. cit.*